THE
DEVIL
HIDES
OUT

THE DEVIL HIDES OUT

New Age and the Occult:
A Christian perspective

DAVID MARSHALL

AUTUMN

HOUSE

ABOUT THE AUTHOR

David Marshall has authored a number of books, among them Christian bestsellers, *Where Jesus Walked* and *The Battle for the Book*.

Dr. Marshall gained first degrees and a PhD from one of Britain's older universities and undertook his doctoral studies under the tutelage of Professor J. P. Kenyon. He is a teacher and author, and a committed evangelical.

He was encouraged to undertake this Christian exposé of the occult — in its various manifestations — by David Watson when rector of St. Michael-le-Belfrey, York. The author's strong stand against the occult and the New Age Movement was influenced by American broadcaster and author, George Vandeman, and by the preaching and writings of Dr. John Stott, rector emeritus of All Souls, Langham Place.

David Marshall is married, part of a large 'three-tier' family and lives in Lincolnshire.

© DAVID MARSHALL, 1991

First published 1991

ISBN 0-904748-57-X

Autumn House Publications
Printed and bound by
The Stanborough Press Ltd.
Alma Park, Grantham, NG31 9SL, England

THE DEVIL HIDES OUT

CONTENTS

HIDDEN WARFARE

A word, for starters, from David Watson . . .

'The marked increase in satanic activity. Not too long ago, the devil's doings were kept pretty much below the surface of civilized society's consciousness.

'Now all that has changed.

'A widespread and intense interest in occult powers and practices confronts us everywhere. School and college students use ouija boards and tarot cards seriously. Sophisticated society people attend seances. Popular magazines feature articles about black and white magic and profile the lives of well-known seers and prophets. Newspapers provide daily astrology readings and a broad coverage of cults that worship Satan.

'In England alone, one recent report estimated that there were 2,500 practising witches, and in the United States some churches have had to keep their doors locked or guarded during the week to prevent devil cultists from sneaking in to perform blasphemous mock communion rites on Christian altars.

'Such realities make obvious the urgent need for Christians to be better equipped for all-out war on Satan.'

DAVID WATSON

HIDDEN WARFARE, STL BOOKS.
Used with permission of Send The Light, PO Box 48, Bromley, Kent, BR1 3JH

UPFRONT

Let's get one thing clear from the off.

I do not swallow hook, line, wing-of-bat and tongue-of-newt every story of the paranormal served up by the tabloid press. Let's face it, exorcisms and things that go bump in the night are the stuff of penny-catching journalism.

Similarly I balk at the storylines of many of the through-weird-to-wonderful-type testimonies you can pick up between paper covers in some Christian bookshops. (More especially if there is far more of the weird than the wonderful about them. . . .) The sort that make the small hairs bristle, the mouth go dry and, ten minutes after you are abed, cause you to flick on the light to make absolutely certain that the shape at the end of your bed really *is* the shirt you have hung out to wear tomorrow! The God we worship is a God of power, love, compassion and grace. What would we be left to think of Him if He allowed His friends to be terrified and tormented by frighteners from the devil's nightmare dimension?

But, on the other hand . . . and, of course, I should not be writing this book if there were not an *other hand* . . . I'm obliged to take seriously the evidence announced to the House of Commons by Geoffrey Dickens, Conservative MP for Littleborough and Saddleworth. A plethora of evidence, in fact, of a new witchcraft craze — yes, you read right: *witchcraft* — and its correlation with the upsurge in the sexual abuse of children.

Much as I might like to, I dare not overlook the findings of Kevin Logan's research — he is vicar of St. John's, Blackburn — on the prevalence and shattering results of occult dabbling among teenagers.

I cannot help but be chilled by what social worker Dianne

Core of Childwatch and her team have turned up on the prevalence and nature of Satanism and its mind-bending, sanity-destroying effect on the hundreds of adolescents interviewed.

My own foot-thick drop file labelled 'Occult' contains documentary evidence that millions in Western countries — Johanna Michaelsen says 65 million in the USA alone — are involved in occult practices from tarot cards and ouija boards to astrology, the obija, witchcraft and outright Satan worship.

Perhaps, above all, the ubiquity of New Age beliefs, practices and attendant paranormal phenomena oblige me to strike a blow for the religion of Jesus Christ (of which the New Age is, in vital respects, the antithesis).

And then there are the millions of the bereaved who, at the time of maximum vulnerability, choked by grief, have fallen prey to the impersonation game that is Spiritualism. . . .

In short, against both education and instinct, I am obliged to face the fact that 'there are more things in heaven and earth' than are dreamt of in the philosophy of the average upwardly-mobile materialist catching the 8.14am to Euston. Then, having faced the fact, I am duty bound both to expose the hazards of the evil unseen world and, by contrast, to present the antidote in the glorious Gospel of freedom in Jesus Christ.

As our exposé gets under way let us keep in mind the words of C. S. Lewis in *Screwtape Letters*:

'There are equal and opposite errors into which our race can fall about devils. One is to disbelieve in their existence. The other is to believe and to feel an excessive and unhealthy interest in them. They themselves are equally pleased by both errors and hail a materialist or a magician with the same delight.'

CHAPTER ONE

SPOOKS, SPECTRES AND THINGS THAT GO BUMP IN THE NIGHT

Greta lay in intensive care. The function of her lungs had been taken over by a life-support machine. Outdoors it was a quiet, November, monochrome day, and clergyman Kevin Logan was having difficulty keeping his temper. He was in the hospital grounds with Greta's guru, Esoteric Mike.

Mike was making the going. 'He's all around! He's in us! He *is* everything!' said the New Age channeller. 'The god-force is not outside of us. It's within us.'

'Oh yes,' said Kevin, 'Greta reached within herself all right. . . .'

'We need to explore "inner space",' persisted Mike un-hearing, 'using the crafts; Transcendental Meditation, trance-channelling. Yes, and drugs. Why not?'

'Look where it's got Greta,' urged Kevin. 'Twenty-three, one of the bonniest lasses I ever saw, kept alive by a machine. . . .'

Typical of London's human flotsam and jetsam, Greta had become a drifter after cutting loose from home. That was six years ago now. Somewhere between Euston station and a temporary job in Virgin Megastore she had run across a New Age set. Its guru: Esoteric Mike.

At first she had mistaken them for Christians. But Greta's first exposure to channelling had blown that one away. Each member of the group had a 'spirit-companion' that dictated life-style and spoke through them when — through drugs or some meditation technique — a trance had been induced.

Hash helped fascination to replace horror, and soon

Greta was experimenting with tarot, astral projection, hypnotic regression . . . anything, in fact, that the revered guru tossed up.

Soon she was reading Shirley Maclaine; 'You will decree what is good for you and you will decree what is evil. . . . If you are god you don't have to be bound by anyone else's convictions but your own. Whatever feels good, do it. . . .'

And, for a time, Greta had taken her advice. . . .

Seeking 'the god-within' and 'self-realization' it seemed great. 'The Age of Pisces, the Age of the Christians', said Mike, 'is finished. The Age of Aquarius has dawned. A New World order is round the corner. . . .'

Mike had led Greta through the soft-occult of the New Age. Then, gradually, witchcraft and Satanism had come to seem acceptable. Soon the hard-core occult had swallowed her up. Somewhere in the promiscuous sex and child-abuse voyeurism at the Satanist temple, Greta had lost all sense of self-worth. And been diagnosed HIV positive.

Then 'the god-within' and the whole weird demi-world of the occult had not seemed to be worth much. To fill her 'inner space' she had swallowed a massive overdose. . . .

In the hospital grounds Esoteric Mike was now talking to himself. A signal from the hospital entrance had extracted Kevin Logan from this painful interview. He strode purposefully across the green sward to the great glass doors.

The crisis for Greta had arrived.

Occult magazines. It was an attempt to make conversation with my newsagent: 'Which of these magazines sells best?' His answer bowled me over: 'Occult magazines. No question. They buy them like there's no tomorrow. My best customers are your students. . . .'

Twenty years ago I was a teacher. Tactful enquiries brought to light the ritual burning of a ouija board. The boarding students had decided to dabble a bit for themselves, watched the glasses move in response to their questions, heard a non-human voice speak out of the ether — and been scared witless. I checked with my newsagent a day or two later. He had experienced a catastrophic decline in the demand for occult magazines. . . .

But, as Time-Life and any major publisher will confirm, my newsagent's downturn in demand for occult publications bucked the trend. For twenty years the number of occult publications in circulation in Western countries has expanded to unbelievable proportions.

The occult has proved a rich seam for the thriller writers. Demand would seem to be insatiable.

We have the word of Nancy Reagan's astrologer, Joan Quigley, that the Reagan White House never made a move without consulting her first. . . . And those who laughed loudest at the Reagans had, doubtless, themselves consulted their horoscope before setting out to work. The Breakfast TV and tabloid astrologers have become household names. Anne Owen 'the woman with the X-ray eyes' had shot to star-status.

TV chat show hosts tumble over each other to get the latest psychic wonder worker to drop in for an interview. Occasionally there is an attempt to be objective. On Hallowe'en one personable interviewer presented three 'experts' to consider the significance of All Hallow's Eve. One was a Bible-believing Christian, the second a 'Christian philosopher' who seemed to believe anything provided it was not in the Bible, and the third was a 'white witch'. Tired of predictable Christians, the interviewer gave two-thirds of the time available to the white witch. The straight Christian got just a single look-in; in one sentence he managed to warn teenagers of the dangers of occult involvement. It was the 'white witch' who cut him off. She agreed with him! 'It's not something I would encourage teenagers to get involved in. It's very dangerous.'

The occult and the media. 'Hallowe'en is the innocent face of the occult,' said a spokesman for the Evangelical Alliance on the TV News. 'Christians should set the day aside to unite in prayer against these growing dangers. On

31 October witches, Satanists and other occult followers will be active. Christians need to strike out in prayer against these dark forces.' He was, it turned out, an English bishop who had conducted a detailed study into occultism among teenagers in England's North-East. In one metropolitan district he had found that 87 per cent of teenagers had experimented with the occult.

On the same day NBC put out a documentary tracing teenage fascination with the occult to a much earlier enthusiasm — for children's television! 'For twenty-five years now', said one authority, 'we have been laughing at the cute antics of Samantha, the 'good' witch on *Bewitched*, and Jeanie, the genie-in-the-bottle in *I Dream of Jeanie*. After-school specials and stories for children are filled with tales of ghosts and goblins and of good little girls and boys learning to become witches and wizards. . . .'

The 70s and 80s saw a long string of big-screen box-office megabuck-makers with occult themes. It all began when producer Noel Marshall and his film star wife, Tippi Hedron, made millions out of all-time block-buster, *The Exorcist* (though it is interesting that an unrelieved catalogue of disasters, including floods, fires, big-cat maulings and serious accidents, has dogged them ever since it made the cinema screens, and that they have now lost the millions they made . . .). But that has not served to deter the same film company from following it up with *Exorcist II, Exorcist III, Omen I* and *Omen II*. And they were just the beginning. . . .

The Alien grossed even more megamillions at the box office. As a video it has done even better. When film critic Tom Davies went to preview it he wrote, 'It is one of the most satanic eruptions of the romantic imagination it has been my misfortune to have seen. Even a week later its effects are beating around, bat-like, in my mind. . . . For much of the film I was under the seat and, for the rest, I gazed, horrified, through a fretwork of fingers and hair.'

Notwithstanding, the demand for videos blending occultism and sex increases by the year. *Nightmare on Elm Street*

(I, II, and III), *The Thing, Aliens* (sequel to *Alien*), *Demons, Evil Dead, The Demonologist, Amityville Horror* (I and II), *The Antichrist, The Exorcist's Daughter, The Demons* and *The Legions of Lucifer*: these are aimed to lure the susceptible into the mind-warping world of the occult through the human psyche's apparent appetite for stark terror.

Best-seller ratings. Stark terror, sex and Satanism is a potent mix in the paperback Top Ten on a typical month.

And not all the occult thrillers purport to be fiction. All over the place there are channellers and mediums eager to tell all about their spirit-populated world. Others write biographies about life-times spent predicting disease, death and disaster — occasionally correctly. Most claim to be able to communicate with the dead.

Once you become aware of it, it is alarming how much media space and time is given over to the occult. And by occult I mean the whole ghoulish bag of tricks: seances, UFOs, New Age, Satanism, black magic, white magic — the whole kit and caboodle dignified by the phrase 'psychic phenomena'. *Elvis Speaks. Dead rock king contacts seance:* the 'spirit' of Presley reportedly spoke through a world-renowned psychic.

Investigative journalism at one stage seemed to be taking on a new dimension. At the invitation of one newspaper 'four leading psychic mediums' held a seance with a view to posing one or two unanswered questions to the 'spirit' of Mary Jo Kopechne who, in the flesh, drowned at Chappaquiddick in an accident which involved Edward Kennedy. In an eerie mirror-lined room, lit by flickering candles, the four psychics held hands, each with a goblet of purified water in front of them. The seance was led by Mrs. Micki Dahne who claims to have had a number of 'conversations' with dead celebrities. The candles flickered dramatically despite the stillness of the air, and Mrs. Dahne stiffened, slumped, and began to speak in what those present believed to be the nasal, New Jersey twang of Mary Jo. (As far as the content of her 'message to the world' was concerned, it might just as well have been the voice of the Kennedy publicity machine absolving the ageing senator from all responsibility in the affair.)

Church concern. Responsible Christian leaders are deeply concerned about the burgeoning fascination with the occult.

Roger Ellis has written *The Occult and Young People* (Kingsway) to warn against 'witches, horoscopes, ouija boards, reincarnation'. He is concerned that his young readers be aware 'of the dangers of dabbling with forces beyond our control'.

Audrey Harper's *Dance with the Devil* (Kingsway) has shocked many Christians out of their complacency. From her own involvement with black witchcraft Mrs. Harper provides detailed and compelling evidence that child abuse is an integral part of the ritual and that those involved have grossed vast sums by procuring children and making pornographic videos for paedophiles.

In *The Seduction of Christianity* (Harvest House), Dave Hunt and T. A. McMahon warn of the extent to which the Christian church has been infiltrated with occult concepts and practices.

At ground level Christians of all persuasions express deep concern.

Recently in Jerusalem I spoke to the Moderator of the Church of Scotland and two of his senior clergy. They were deeply disturbed by the power of the occult in parts of Scotland, including Edinburgh. There was talk of spiritualist phenomena, even devil possession.

A senior clergyman wrote to me from North Wales. The ministry of every Christian denomination in Rhyl, Colwyn Bay and Llandudno were uniting together in a day of prayer and preaching against the occult. In a Wales-wide BBC radio and TV link-up my correspondent had said: 'North Wales is a centre of witchcraft, spiritualism and other occult practices. . . .'

Dr. Michael Green, an Anglican, records that at a meeting of Nottinghamshire clergy, 'I did not find one who had not had some recent experience of the occult in his pastoral work.' He goes on: 'During five years in supposedly sophisticated Oxford, I saw more of it than in the previous eighteen years of ministry.'

But, on the other side of the coin, churchmen have not been above the lure of the occult. There has been the case of Bishop James Pike who, after spooky goings-on in his flat in Cambridge, sought out medium Arthur Ford and, in a televised seance, allegedly talked with his suicide son. In letters to the London *Times*, Mervyn Stockwood, then Bishop of Southwark, announced that on five occasions he had communicated with the dead. There are Anglican bishops among the patrons of the Churches' Fellowship for Psychical and Spiritual Studies.

So, what are we to make of it all?

In his classic *The Occult*, Colin Wilson writes: 'Ever since the 1880s the Society of Psychical Research has been collecting evidence of various kinds of "psychic" experiences, and some of it is very convincing indeed. It may not prove life after death, *but it proves that something very odd is going on*.'

All of which begs an obvious question. If 'something very odd is going on' what on earth (or elsewhere) is it?

When Kevin Logan reached Intensive Care the monitors and digital dials no longer flickered. The robotic click of the ventilator had ceased. Greta was dead. The occult had claimed another victim.

CHAPTER TWO

AN ALIEN FORCE

Les was everyone's all-purpose villain. In the studio they kept him at arm's length. He had not a fluid ounce of social oil. Invariably surly, he could at times be downright nasty.

Les went around with the motorbike gang. Long after lights out in suburbia, the screech and roar of their powerful machines split the comfortable dreams of a community. Nor was their kamikaze road-style modified when one of their number, Jeff, left his life-blood on the radiator of a passing juggernaut.

Les thought he was Jack-the-Lad. He needed nobody. Among his workmates in the studio, Barry was the only one who tried to make conversation. But, more often than not, he was told to save his breath for blowing his porridge. Then it all changed. One morning.

Les turned up late for work. Nothing unusual in that. But his face was ashen white. His gait had lost its swagger. The old Jack-the-Lad style had all gone. He had aged half a life-time overnight and, despite strenuous efforts to control himself, his body shook.

'What's up, Mate?' asked Barry, taken aback. There was a heavy silence.

'*Been to see the vicar,*' said Les.

The comment would have been more credible if he'd said, 'Been on a pound-stretcher to Venus.'

Les and his entire gang had lived through a mind-warping experience.

Always involved in a desperate search for kicks the gang had acquired a *ouija* board. On this board the letters of the alphabet and the signs of the zodiac were arranged in a semicircle with the words 'yes' and 'no' at either end. A glass was turned upside-down and each participant placed one finger on the glass. The 'spirit of the glass' was then asked to move it in answer to a question.

The gang had heard all about ouija boards being 'spooked', and some of the weird tales people told about them. They were determined to give it a go. Sitting in a leather-jacketed phalanx across the back row of the local Odeon they had guffawed their way through a score of horror films that would have scared the average fellow witless. Nothing could frighten *them*. They'd seen it all. Ghostly faces at windows. Shadowy phantoms from the chambers of death. Spectral figures rising from tombs on nights when lightning slashed the sky in angry stabs. It was all done by the special-effects men. Now they wanted to throw down a challenge to any spirit-world that might exist. They wanted some home-made horror.

And they got it.

The glass *did* move in answer to their questions.

But that left them only slightly unnerved. Though everyone swore they were not cheating, there was always an outside chance. . . . The answers given to their questions, they began to realize, could not have come from *their* heads, but then again it was just possible that. . . . As they continued, an unmistakable atmosphere of evil began to pervade the room, weighing them down, hanging heavily in the air. It felt as if the dirty room with its boxes and refuse and empty jars and milk bottles and all manner of putrefaction was filled with far more people than the gang of lads around the table with their fingers on a glass that was moving around, it seemed, of its own volition, however light the touch of their fingers. . . . Each wondered if it was all in the imagination. . . . Each darted a furtive glance at the faces of the others — and saw the same terror reflected in everyone's eyes. . . .

Beads of sweat sprang from their foreheads. Heads and arms and whole bodies began to quiver, then shake, almost convulse.

There was a tremendous sound. The glass shattered. The

contents of the room moved, and shook. It felt as if a high-speed train was passing through. . . .

Or, perhaps, a juggernaut. . . .

But this was Hammersmith. They weren't at the Odeon. There were no special-effects men.

Fantasy had gate-crashed reality.

It was actually going on.

And worse was to come.

Shaking most violently were three empty milk bottles. The attention of the lads fastened on them, terror-riven.

Then there was a voice. It came from somewhere in the area of the milk bottles. And the voice was — or at least *seemed* to be — unmistakable.

But Jeff was dead.

They had seen the mangled remains of the body and the bike. Jeff was undoubtedly dead.

Above the din and the clatter Jeff's voice was speaking. . . . It was Jeff. The distinctive high-pitched tones of Jeff. . . .

A voice from the dead?

In that instant, Les told Barry — hours later, but still shaking and still ashen-white in the commercial art studio they shared — one thought pounced into the mind of each member of the gang: *move it!* Priority one: put space between themselves and that room — and whatever alien force had entered it at their invitation.

At what time this occurred, Les didn't say. So we don't know how much time the gang spent driving around on those high-powered bikes before morning.

One thing is certain. The first light of dawn found these lads on the doorstep of an Anglican clergyman — in search of counsel and answers to a lot of questions.

Equally certain is that, come 9am, Les, fear quivering in his normally brazen features, was telling his tale to Barry.

And Barry has just told the tale to me.

What do I make of it?

I should like to be able to say that I don't believe a word of it. For a great many reasons it would give me satisfaction to do so. But I can't. Even making allowance for exaggeration, I cannot dismiss the story as the product of a frenetic imagination.

Why?

Because I have heard too many stories like it.

So what is this terrifying alien force that reduced a gang of mucho machos to jelly?

CHAPTER THREE

THE CURIOUS CASE OF THE HAUNTED BISHOP

Bishop James Pike was one of those clerics the media love to feature. As the great Christian festivals come round — Christmas, Easter, Whitsun — they feel obliged to come up with some sort of 'religious' story. Bishop Pike could always be depended on to air his unbelief on these occasions, and to provide a quotable quote or, if they really got lucky, an 'in-depth' interview.

For one thing Bishop Pike didn't believe in life after death. That much everyone knew.

But one day, quite suddenly, he changed his mind. And the events that brought about that change of mind were emblazoned across the North American media scene though, in fact, they began in the Bishop's flat in Cambridge.

There had always been something a bit strange about the Bishop's son Jim. When the Bishop and his family stayed with Johanna Michaelsen's parents in Mexico, Johanna described 17-year-old Jim as having a 'dark, brooding air which could erupt easily into violence'. But, taken as a package, Johanna thought Jim and his younger brother Chris were 'typical preacher's kids'. Other Jim-watchers were a touch less charitable; they said that he was so insensitive that he was bullet-proof!

But bullet-proof or no, Jim Pike, son of the well-known, well-larded writer and bishop, was not proof against his own life-style.

On 4 February 1966 Jim Pike committed suicide in a New York hotel room. It was down to drugs, said the coroner. Bishop Pike was especially distressed. Not long before, he and Jim had spent — in Cambridge — the most harmonious period of their father-son relationship.

But it was not young Jim's death that changed the Bishop's views about life after death. It was the psychic phenomena that broke out in his Cambridge flat *following* Jim's death.

No sooner had Jim's body been cremated and his ashes scattered over the Pacific than a series of events occurred in the flat the Bishop had shared with his son that made the ageing cleric's heart do handstands. Resident with the grief-stricken Bishop in the flat at the time of the occurrences were David Barr, his chaplain, and Maren Bergrud, his secretary.

Young Jim had been a great collector of postcards. He bought them wherever he went. Inexplicably two of these postcards were standing on the Bishop's dressing-table one night — *placed at a 140 degree angle*.

Two days later Maren Bergrud looked in the morning mirror with both anger and consternation. Someone, in the night, had cut off part of her fringe! Apparently with a pair of scissors!

Revd Barr, part serious, part confused, remarked that Jim had never liked her fringe. . . .

It was the day after that that things took an ugly turn. Maren awoke with a cry of pain, a gallon of adrenalin surging through her veins. Two of her fingernails had been injured as if a sharp, pointed knife had been stuck underneath them. Her emotions in mutinous disorder, her mouth sand-dry, she rushed to the bathroom to wrap some elastoplast round her fingers. When she sat down to breakfast David Barr, now somewhat unnerved himself, said, 'Maren, the rest of your fringe has been cut off!'

Taking it all in, the Bishop stooped forward and sighed as he steepled his fingers. Maren looked at him quietly, expecting some kind of comment, because the morning's revelations were not over. When no comment was forthcoming Maren told the Bishop of another weird event.

On the previous evening the Bishop had gone to bed early.

After he had fallen asleep Maren had remembered that part of his manuscript she had been meant to be working on had been left on his bedside table. She had tiptoed into the darkened room. The Bishop had been sitting bolt upright in bed, staring into space. A voice, not *his* voice, had been speaking through him, and ideas — not his but Jim's — had been articulated by the voice.

The Bishop, his fastidious, aged face as pale as a silver coin, could remember nothing of this. But David Barr, his voice quavering, said that he had awoken the previous night in an atmosphere of bleak, suicidal depression. (The sort of mood, in fact, Jim might have experienced after one of his drug trips. . . .)

The three of them went to London for the day. Subconsciously, perhaps, the Bishop was looking for something to staunch the internal bleeding of his melancholy. They returned to Cambridge just after 4pm. There was a stillness, and a clothy weight to the sky that hid the sun. When they re-entered the flat they were met by a whole array of strange phenomena.

On the Bishop's dressing table, in place of the two postcards, were two books — at the same 140 degree angle. Two photographs of Jim and his father had been removed from the Bishop's mirror; they were later to be discovered in a heap of old clothes at the bottom of a wardrobe. Unfamiliar blank stationery was found, and more postcards.

And there was something strange about the living room clock. For weeks it had been stuck at 12.15. Now it read 8.19. This meant that the clock hands formed the same enigmatic 140 degree angle as the cards and the books. It struck Barr first: it was Cambridge time for Jim's death in New York.

This was the day when, quite suddenly, the Bishop changed his views on life after death. Previously he had not believed it possible in any form. Now he began to believe in the after life as a shadowy realm of spirits. More and more he was drawn into the perilous world of the occult.

There were more strange happenings in the flat. Venetian blinds closed as Jim would have closed them. Heat turned up as Jim would have liked it. One morning all the milk in the fridge, including what had been delivered that morning, had turned sour.

David Barr and Maren Bergrud were way ahead of the Bishop in their belief in the occult. Upon their advice he consulted the well-known spiritualist medium Ena Twigg. A seance was set up.

On the day immediately prior to the one planned for the seance there were more strange happenings. Windows opened by themselves, books and clothes moved about, safety-pins scattered around (arranged in the 140 degree angle) and a partly-smoked cigarette was found on the Bishop's dressing-table (Jim's brand).

The Bishop's fear had seemingly evaporated. In its place was fascination. He was positively excited as Ena Twigg, Maren (present to take notes) and he himself began the seance. Ena went into a trance, as anticipated; and then announced that Jim was present in the room. She proceeded to give his message. Bishop Pike felt exhilarated. Never having been able to accept the miraculous aspect of Christian belief — including the virgin birth, the divinity of Christ and the resurrection — he had apparently no difficulty at all in accepting that 'the presence' he felt in the seance room was that of his son.

A second seance with Ena Twigg was set up. In the course of the consultation Bishop Pike asked for the name of a reputable American medium. While in a trance Mrs. Twigg mentioned 'Spiritual Frontiers'. This meant nothing to the Bishop at the time. However, she *was* able to assure him that Jim would next be 'in touch' with his father in August.

Bishop Pike crossed the Atlantic. He was given a number of preaching engagements. One was in New York. It was attended by Arthur Ford, then one of America's foremost mediums. The service over, Ford approached the Bishop. He told him that while he had been preaching there had been two figures behind him. One had been Jim and the other had been Elias. Again Pike was fascinated; How could Ford possibly have known that Jim's maternal grandfather was called Elias? Arthur Ford soon cleared up the 'Spiritual Frontiers' conundrum. It was the name of his organization.

August found Bishop Pike attending to his duties in his diocese — California. On 1 August he learned that a Spiritual Frontiers medium was in his area. He telephoned him immediately. The medium told him that he had been expecting his call. Jim had, apparently, been in contact with the medium two weeks previously.

Five seances followed in which Bishop Pike allegedly spoke to his son and 'saw' something that he took to be his son. The news swept America. Media moguls wanted more of the story; they wanted to be on the inside. The Canadian Broadcasting Corporation suggested another seance, this time with Arthur Ford himself. Ford readily agreed, as did the Bishop. There followed the famous televised seance seen throughout Canada and parts of the United States.

By now James Pike was as caught up in the murky world of the occult as was Arthur Ford himself. It held an irresistible fascination for him. Strange, really. He had always prided himself on his logic. His formula had been 'facts plus faith'. The facts, in this case, he said, were the psychic phenomena. And the faith? For the first time in his life he was not short of that.

Not long after, Bishop Pike died in the Judaean wilderness searching for the 'historical' Jesus. His wife, Diane, back in a Jerusalem's King David hotel, reported to the waiting newsmen that she had seen it all in a vision. She had watched his spirit leave his body, rise above the jaws of a wadi — and ascend to heaven. Here, she said, her husband was greeted by his old friend Paul Tillich — and Jim. Of this 'strange reunion' George Vandeman comments: 'A bishop who did not believe in Christ. A suicide son who wanted a religion that does not "force God and Jesus down one's throat". And Paul Tillich, the renowned theologian who was called "the father of the death-of-God school''. Yet all arrive in heaven.' *Psychic Roulette* (Nelson), page 19.

The Bishop had believed in facts plus faith. And he accepted the psychic phenomena uncritically as 'facts'.

Up to a point, of course, he was right. The psychic phenomena were 'facts' in the sense that they really happened. But did Jim have anything to do with them?

Would it not have been wiser for Bishop Pike to have tackled the problem of the psychic phenomena in his flat with a little more detachment? Unquestionably, 'something very odd was going on'. In the Bishop's terms that was a 'fact'. Did he go wrong in his identification of what the 'odd' phenomena represented?

The last twenty years have seen an acceleration of feedback from the world of the unseen. Man is tossing balls across the wall to the unseen world. Somebody, apparently, is tossing them back. Who? And is it dangerous? Is it safe to initiate the game without knowing the identity of the opposing player?

We are surrounded by a psychic cinerama. Recently the Committee for the Scientific Investigation of Claims of the Paranormal held its annual conference at Stanford University. Essentially they are sceptics; 'America must have the lushest undergrowth of weird credos . . . ,' said a spokesman. And of course they are right to be sceptical about Uri Geller's tricks, in the influence of Scorpio, Mars, Pluto and Uranus (and the rest) on everyday life, on the Bermuda Triangle and crop circles and a lot else beside.

But, in dismissing the obvious frauds, are they turning their backs on the all-too-well-authenticated paranormal phenomena? And, in doing so, are they guilty of the opposite error from Bishop Pike? The evidence adduced by ultra-sceptical John Hick in *Death and Eternal Life* (MacMillan) with regard to psychic phenomena oblige us to accept that 'deliberate fraud' can 'for all practical purposes be excluded in the best cases of trancemediumship'. In short: I respect the efforts of the 'ghostbusters' — and I wish I could believe what they say — but the evidence obliges me to accept that psychic phenomena *do* take place and that, as far as the assorted psychics and mediums (and their clients) are concerned, the whole business is very, very serious indeed.

The weird and eerie world of the occult seems to be a huge submerged magnet pulling the explorer into it, and demanding verification by the physical senses.

Man likes the psychic ball game even if he doesn't know the identity of his opposing team. Is this attitude safe?

Even Ruth Montgomery, a medium of mediums, answers that question with an emphatic, No. Why? 'You are', she writes, 'opening a door through which mischievous or malevolent spirits might enter.'

Medium Brenda Crenshaw writes: 'A person who wants to become a medium must realize the tremendous responsibility which this places upon him and also realize that there are dangers in it as well. There are spirits on the other side who are willing to come back to a medium and take possession of him. . . . There are spirits who are impersonators and will come back through a medium and make claims that are not true.'

Psychic ice, evidently is perilously thin. Even the psychics say that. And they ought to know.

Diane Pike, Bishop Pike's widow, writes that she once asked her husband if he had considered the possibility that he might be involved with the world of evil spirits. His reply had been that the thought had crossed his mind, but that it was too disturbing and that he had buried it. . . .

The question remains: Man is tossing balls across the wall of the unseen world. And somebody is tossing them back. Who?

We owe it to ourselves to find out.

CHAPTER FOUR

SPIRIT VISITORS

Kate and Keith married at 20. Kate had never had eyes for anyone but Keith. And Keith, though acutely aware that his girl was, in some sense, 'strange', went into marriage with the enthusiasm of any normal young man. And normal he was, and is. Keith has a quick wit, a balanced outlook and two feet set decisively on *terra firma*.

Kate first became aware of her 'strange powers' at 14. In dreams, night after night, she felt a warm wind pass across her face and found herself staring into the candle-fat features of a 'living' corpse. In repeated nightmares this apparition showed her scenes and gave her information that alarmed her. But when, in the daytime world of fact and flesh, a fair few of the scenes and predictions became real, smug self-satisfaction replaced fear. Kate's night-time visitor, with an above-evens degree of precision, was showing her things that would happen in the future. On a number of occasions young Kate was told of deaths before they happened. Her parents told her that her grandmother and her great aunt possessed a similar 'power'.

One night Kate's nightmare was particularly vivid. She was watching the dark sea's swell; its salt-bitter passion, its swinging, definite motion, its strength, its attack. Then a huge hand emerged from the sea. It grasped the form of a boy and dragged him under. Kate heard the nerve-tensing scream of a woman, shrill, uncontrolled.

The next day Kate's cousin, on holiday in Florida, was drowned. His mother witnessed the drowning and screamed hysterically for a long period.

Kate was secretly proud of her strange powers. There was no obvious connection with evil, though there was an un-canny preoccupation with death and darkness. She saw no clash between her Methodist background and her extra-sensory 'gift'.

Not long after marrying Keith, Kate had her first 'spirit visitation'. She described the 'spirit' to her mother. Nervously her mother told her that she had seen her long-dead great-grandmother.

That night Kate's grandfather died suddenly.

Keith didn't like the sound of this. He tried to distance himself from this whole area of Kate's life. But this became increasingly difficult. Kate's friends were fascinated by the weird happenings in her home.

One night Kate and Keith had a few friends round. The conversation turned to the supernatural. They wanted to 'try something'. Keith immediately announced his intention of going to bed. With Keith out of the way the others gathered around the table. Letters were arranged out of sequence. Questions were addressed by Kate to the spirit world. The letters began to be rearranged into words by invisible hands.

Then one of the men, absorbed in the proceedings, was struck a blow to the head which sent him reeling. No one could possibly have administered the blow. Then another man was severely hit.

The party broke up.

Kate just laughed.

As the months went by she discovered that she could read tarot cards. Keith was sickened by the eager little groups who would hunch around the table. His spine tingled when a fair average of Kate's 'fortunes' came true.

By now Kate saw herself as a medium. She organized 'sittings'. The ritual was of her own devising. Alien voices spoke through her. Apparitions manifested themselves. . . .

As time went on it became impossible to believe that the source of the supernatural happenings was good. Keith had never had any illusions; but Kate also became aware of an all-pervasive evil in the home into which they had moved after marriage. It weighed them down and induced depression. Occasionally at first, and then with increasing frequency, it terrified.

There were knockings on doors in the darkness. Feet walked the stairs and in the upstairs rooms. Objects moved about. Tricks were played with the electrical system; even the washing machine could move from one side of the room to the other — and turn itself on.

One night Kate, Keith and their baby daughter Carol were sitting silently in the living-room. Was it the weeping night outside which steeped the room in a sepulchral gloom? Or was there an unseen presence which made heartbeats hammer, flesh tingle and small hairs bristle? Eyes registered fear near to terror. The baby stared, wide-eyed as babies are not wont to do. Burly Keith's palms were sweating.

A violent noise split the silence. It was right outside the living-room door. It was as if a wild beast was banging, clawing at the door. The aura of indescribable, ultimate evil filled the room. The depression which had so long weighed Kate down brought her to hysteria. Flesh quivering, Keith stood up. He moved to the door.

He opened it.

There was nothing there.

The noise ceased on the instant. But the aura of evil remained.

Terror-crazed by the atmosphere that pervaded the house, Keith and Kate made plans to move. Kate's depression had gone beyond all bounds of endurance. Keith himself was miserable.

Their new home was modern, light. But Kate had brought the evil with her. A rift was developing between Kate and Keith. Little Carol, small as she was, became more and more difficult to control, until control became impossible. Keith wept inwardly as he saw what was happening to the wife and child he loved.

Their relationship was not helped when Kate announced to Keith that his mother was going to die. On a still, dead evening when no twig stirred, the couple sat quietly in their living-room, curtains drawn.

Suddenly the room was filled with an atmosphere of evil.

What looked like an old man appeared with the hollow eyes of a hermit.

That night Keith's mother died.

Kate began to experiment with regression. There was no shortage of friends eager to participate. Under the influence of a form of hypnotism Kate took them back into their past lives. It seemed like fun.

But now Kate was being drawn into unspeakable evil. Her language was so foul as to be devil-spoken. She became a compulsive liar and thief.

Kate also became an adulteress.

She had loved no man in her life but Keith, nor did she do so now. But she was being drawn by an evil force from which there seemed to be no escape. She left her lovely home, handsome, attentive husband, and her little daughter, and moved with another man to a town some sixty miles distant.

She says now that she had not wanted to leave. And that the evil things that she did, she had not wanted to do.

Chronic depression which by now had afflicted her for a number of years, took over. Kate wanted to die. Death was the answer. Suicide, she decided, was best accomplished in a car. On numerous occasions when driving at speed she felt a powerful compulsion to ram a wall or another vehicle. She fought the compulsion. Another force was working within her; a force of light and goodness. Another voice was speaking to her, apart from the hideous chatter of the evil spirits.

One day she made a decision: she wanted death — or she wanted Jesus Christ. The choice had to be made urgently.

For the first time in many years she prayed to her Heavenly Father, a stammering, blurted-out prayer. A peace descended.

Kate returned to her home and to Keith.

She encountered the minister of her old church. 'If I don't find Jesus Christ I'm going to kill myself,' she said. He prayed with her, was sympathetic — and she never saw him again.

Kate tried many denominations. Among them were

Mormons and Jehovah's Witnesses. But she did not find Christ there.

'Lord,' she prayed, 'if you want me at all you must show me the way!'

But if Kate was desperate, the spirits were getting desperate too. On two occasions an apparition appeared to her. It was not a cadaverous form now. It was a man of incredible beauty and magnetism. On both occasions the apparition invited her to murder her husband with a pair of scissors.

But a power for good was at work.

Kate received an invitation to attend a Bible study group organized by the Church of England. She went along. Among those present were representatives of a number of Christian churches. The discussion was marvellous. Her depression was lifted. In conversation with one member of the group she mentioned her search for Christ. He gave her a copy of a magazine entitled *Focus on Jesus Christ*. She took it home and discussed it at length with Keith. She was impressed by the fact that Jesus was at the centre of every article.

A meeting was set up between Kate and a local Christian minister.

But this seemed like a challenge to the spirit world. Kate's problems were by no means over. The night prior to her scheduled meeting with the Christian minister was to be the longest of her life. . . .

There were many questions to which Kate wanted answers. Who were these spirits who, having entered her nightmares, with her encouragement had come to crowd her life and bring with them forecasts of bad news — and mind-warping terror? Was the power of the Jesus of whom she had learned in her Methodist upbringing sufficient to defeat this unseen world of spirits, and lead her beyond it to light and freedom?

CHAPTER FIVE

QUEEN OF THE BLACK WITCHES

'Daring Diana' was well known on the Soho circuit. From prostitution in Paddington, Doreen Irvine — stage name 'Diana' — had graduated to stripping 'up West'.

From the poor corner of the poorest part of the East End, Doreen had been reared the eldest of five sisters. Her father drank his wages and her mother nursed her bruises — until the day she disappeared — for ever. Doreen was just 11.

Next day a 'new mother' was installed with a ready-made family. She added another child annually to the brood Doreen felt duty-bound to look after.

Doreen took to hanging around the local tube station dreaming of freedom. After a number of failed escape attempts she finally succeeded. Lonely, bewildered, she paid a week's rent in advance on a room in Paddington, using the only cash she had brought with her. The next room was rented by six friendly prostitutes. Within twenty-four hours Doreen was 'on the game' — at 14!

Her accession to fame as a stripper had come after answering an advertisement for a 'model'. Her world was populated by bread-heads, hustlers and sugar-daddies. Guilt produced severe bouts of depression. She looked for escape from this house-of-strangers she called life. But, in the whirl of gaudy brilliance and strobed, smoke-filled darkness, screeching music scraping the ears, rational thought was an impossibility.

Hiding her depression under her cockney good-for-a-laugh veneer, Doreen encountered disaster at the dressing-room door. He was a pusher. And, in her depressed state of mind, Doreen was a push *over*. She turned her face away as he tied a tourniquet and injected a shot of heroin in the main vein near her elbow.

She was hooked and, when needing a fix, would crumple up on the club floor wailing hysterically until one of the girls ran to find the pusher.

At first she had plenty of money to pay. But her bank balance was dwindling as the pusher, knowing of Doreen's total dependence, exacted a higher price for every fix.

One night she noticed two girls whispering in one of the clubs. She recollected that they had nothing to do with any of the other girls and seemed to share some big secret. In the smoke-filled darkness she crept up behind them. All she caught was a mention of a Satanists' temple.

When the girls realized they had been overheard they became hostile. Only after a great deal of persuasion were they induced to say a word.

'We are Satanists and worship at the temple of Satan.'

'Can I come too?' asked Doreen.

Arrangements were made. At a pre-arranged place and time a large black car drew up. Before it pulled away from the kerb the driver had blindfolded Doreen.

The blindfold was only removed inside the Satanist temple. It was a large, square hall. She estimated that about 500 were present. Up front was a raised area draped in black. At the centre of it a robed, hooded figure sat on what looked like a throne. In a semicircle around him stood thirteen figures, also robed in black. One of the girls from the club explained that they were the priests and priestesses of the order of Satanism.

The ceremony involved rhythmic chanting which grew louder and louder. The robed figure stood down from the platform. Two of the priests removed his hood. 'That's the chief Satanist,' one of the girls explained. Everyone prostrated themselves in an attitude of worship.

The rhythmic chanting ebbed and flowed. All eyes were on the chief Satanist as he kissed the vessels, the knives and the emblems of Satanism that had been taken from the high altar.

In the absence of artificial light the whole scene was lit by flaming torches. Cockerels were brought in, their necks wrung and their blood spattered everywhere. Then the cockerels were offered to Satan in sacrifice with more chanting.

But if the eyes of everyone were focused on the chief Satanist, *his* eyes were focused on Doreen. She involuntarily shivered.

She was aware of the presence of evil.

The two-hour ceremony over, she was surprised to see the chief Satanist in mufti. He approached her and, in a disarming manner, asked her to join them. The other girls were visibly awed by his interest in Doreen.

Soon she was attending Satanist meetings on a regular basis. She became aware that their location moved from time to time. She witnessed scenes of evil which she was subsequently unprepared to describe. Among the 500 worshippers she encountered bankers, shop-keepers and teachers, as well as prostitutes and drug addicts. Part of the code was complete secrecy. The Bible was not to be read. Indeed, part of Satanic worship was the mockery and burning of Bibles and Christian literature. Satan was to be worshipped in all situations, they were told. He saw all things and must be obeyed. Lying, cheating, free lust — even murder — were condoned. Prayer to Satan was to be made daily.

The chief Satanist became a regular visitor at the strip clubs. In no time Doreen was his mistress. He supplied her heroin and asked no payment. He ordered her to continue prostitution.

At a satanic temple in south London a special ceremony took place. Present were representatives from Satanist temples from all parts of England. Black-robed Doreen was formally sworn in as a child of Satan. Her blood was mixed with that of a white cockerel. She drank some of it, made her vows to Satan and, dipping her finger in the mixed blood, signed a parchment making over her soul to the devil. Doreen was sworn in as a high priestess of Satan. Frenzied scenes of indescribable evil ensued.

Doreen felt, at the same time, unclean — and of great importance. She was conscious of a menacing evil surrounding her, night and day. She slept little, but received supernatural strength to carry on.

From Satanism, her lover led her into black magic. Witchcraft was not practised in temples, but in remote settings such as deserted houses, lonely beaches, or stretches of woodland. 'Black witches and Satanists', writes Doreen Irvine, 'believe that in the ultimate battle between good and evil, evil will triumph. They believe that Lucifer will one day conquer Christ and will retrieve what they call his rightful place.'

Some years later, when Doreen Irvine came to set down these events on paper, she found it impossible to describe the full horror and debauchery practised in the witches' coven. At her initiation goat's blood was smeared over her naked body. Perverted sexuality, sadism, lesbianism and homosexuality were the hallmarks of black witchcraft.

'My powers as a black witch were great, and I added to my knowledge of evil every day,' writes Doreen Irvine. 'My ability to levitate four or five feet was very real. . . . I could make objects appear and disappear. . . .'

'You might even be the queen of the black witches one day, Diana,' said the chief Satanist.

He submitted her name.

A special test of her powers was to be held on Dartmoor, the centre of two large and active covens. In the midst of an obscure ritual the witches became aware that three men were approaching over the brow of a hill. They panicked.

'No problem,' said Doreen. 'I can make myself invisible.'

'But what about us?' they asked.

'Put yourself in my power,' ordered Doreen, 'and I'll make you invisible too.'

They obeyed her orders. Doreen called upon the powers of darkness. The three men could scarcely see one another, let alone the witches. Doreen reached out her hand and touched one of them but he saw nothing.

The following day the local newspaper carried the

headline: 'No witches on Dartmoor.' The report recounted that a local preacher had taken two reporters on to Dartmoor in an attempt to investigate a rumour that witches were to be present. The search had been fruitless. . . .

It was at this point that Doreen had her first shock. She attempted to put a curse on the preacher. Nothing happened to him. 'I had no idea that a far greater power than that of Satan was protecting this man,' wrote Doreen.

Not long after, on Hallowe'en, Dartmoor was to be the hive of black magic activity again. Plymouth hotels were full of guests, the hoteliers unaware that they were witches from Holland, Germany, France and all parts of England — come to witness the coronation of Diana, queen of the witches.

There were no broomsticks outside the hotels; plenty of BMWs and Audis. Drugs were taken before the ceremony on Dartmoor. There were chants to the ancient gods and demons. In the ensuing ceremony Doreen killed a bird in flight — and walked, unscathed, through a great bonfire. It was at this point that Doreen saw him materialize — a great black figure. 'I took his hand and walked with him to the centre of the great blaze. There I paused, the great flames leaping around me. Only when I emerged at the other side of the blaze did my master, Diablos, disappear.'

'Hail, Diana, queen of black witches!' was the cry from the throats of a thousand witches.

She was crowned and cloaked and an orb placed in her hand. She sat on a throne prepared before the ceremony. Frenzied scenes followed, fuelled by drink and drugs.

In the months that followed 'Diana' travelled across Europe with the chief Satanist.

Great convocations came together. There was much discussion. The issue: How to make witchcraft appear a natural, innocent adventure, appealing to a wider public.

Back in England 'Diana' enjoyed significant success, removing some of the sinister trappings that made witchcraft frightening.

'Diana' was queen of the black witches for one year. Then she stepped down to permit a younger person to take the title. As soon as she had done so the chief Satanist found himself a new mistress.

Life became less hectic. Doreen continued to fall back on prostitution to finance her drug habit. Difficult times followed. The passing months brought an increasing fear of ageing, of death. Questions gate-crashed Doreen's mind.

She knew that no one could leave black witchcraft and live.

After a time 'Daring Diana' found herself a prostitute in the St. Paul's district of Bristol. The St. Paul's district, in addition to being the red light quarter of Bristol, also contained many churches.

One day she was brought up with a jolt. It was a placard outside one of Bristol's churches: 'Come and hear Eric Hutchings at Colston Hall.'

Eric Hutchings. The name sounded familiar. And then she remembered. He was the Plymouth preacher who had tried to expose witchcraft on Dartmoor.

To the laughter of the other prostitutes Doreen went around tearing down the posters wherever she found them. Her anger seemed uncontrollable.

She had lived through experiences of evil that beggar description. Even sold her soul to Satan. An iterative voice rang in her memory, '*No way out. No escape.*'

In her book *From Witchcraft to Christ* (Concordia), which has gone through eighteen printings since it was first published, Doreen Irvine tells her story.

She also recounts her way of escape. The route was to be long and tortuous. But a journey which had begun among darkness, depression, drugs and demons was to end in the light of life and the salvation that is to be found in Jesus Christ alone.

CHAPTER SIX

DEVILISH BUSINESS

'Jane' is 21 and living in hiding.

Britain's sober-sides Sunday, *The Observer*, published her account on 16 September 1990. It was at a time when thirty-three children from Rochdale and Manchester had been made wards of court pending investigations into allegations of Satanic ritual abuse.

Jane had been introduced to a coven by her father at the age of 5. On the first occasion, with other children, she had posed nude for a photographer and been told she was a 'clever girl'. On each subsequent visit she had been sexually abused. Frequently she had to remain away from home for a period of days to allow her body to heal.

Men and women participated in a Satanic ritual in which all wore dark robes, their faces partly obscured by a hood. Venues varied from week to week; sometimes a cellar or attic would be used, occasionally 'a hastily-converted living-room'. Jane had been sexually abused as part of a Satanic ritual for fourteen years. Those present had included police officers and professionals and had varied in number from thirteen to 100.

Eighteen months before giving her story to *The Observer*, Jane had made a break. 'She has since moved from safe house to safe house — and been discovered several times. Jane is a low-key person. Her story is backed by her social worker, although police have only now begun to take action,' reads *The Observer*. 'Medical evidence indicates physical and sexual abuse.'

Christopher Brown, director of the NSPCC, has no doubt as to the veracity of Jane's story. He reports an alarming rise in child pornography and sex rings; 'Children throughout Britain are being exploited by abuse which is highly organized and planned.'

Jim Harding, the national child-care officer of the NSPCC, reports that the correlation between the sexual exploitation of children and the increasing incidence of witchcraft and devil worship is 'causing a great deal of anxiety'. Under a headline 'Forced into Satanic Sex Rituals' the *Daily Mail* reports Harding as saying, 'We have been worried about these things for a long time. But we have been cautious about speaking out until we knew more.' Most of the evidence had come from children, he said. But some had come from adults, like Jane, who had been involved in organized sexual abuse when they were younger.

A task-force involving the NSPCC, the Department of Health, the police and welfare organizations has, reported Harding, been set up to investigate the growing number of reported cases of children being subjected to horrendous sexual abuse in the context of Satanic ceremonies.

Glasgow's *Daily Record* had caught the same trend. Child abuse by devil worshippers was happening in Scotland — and was on the increase. Police, social workers and churchmen from all over Scotland had been warned. At a conference in Dundee, Chicago policeman Jerry Simandl and American child-care expert Pamela Klein had said that the children they had examined (in the USA) had first seemed to have been 'routinely' sexually abused. Only afterwards was it discovered that they had been forced to take part in 'nightmare sacrificial ceremonies'.

Klein described the uphill struggle that she and her colleagues had faced in making others believe that the horror stories they were hearing were true; 'Youngsters talked of ghosts and being encouraged to kill babies.'

Beyond the occasional credibility-stretching 'in-depth exposé' of a Wapping tabloid, little serious investigative journalism has taken place on this subject. The first magazine to take an interest was up-market *She*. The findings of *She* reporter Bill Williamson received a little attention in *The Observer* and *The Guardian*, and his more sensational findings found a bowdlerized treatment in the tabloids.

She sent Williamson to investigate readers' stories of resurgence of the black arts, bizarre Satanic rituals, sex, drugs and child sacrifice. 'Were these stories the product of an over-active imagination,' Williamson wanted to know, 'or were we really in the grip of a sinister and murderous trend?'

His conclusion?

'We look at the startling evidence around us and discover that in contemporary Britain, Satan is alive and well, and his disciples are actively recruiting followers. . . .

'For every poorly-researched and sensationalized tabloid shock-horror Satanist story there is a genuine article. . . .'

Williamson's research began when he interviewed John Merry, a tough newshound who had been scenting down the sexual abuse of children in the North-East.

Before long MP Geoffrey Dickens had come alongside with a mountain of evidence linking the veritable epidemic of Satanism with the climbing statistics for child molestation — and even murder.

Then Williamson had found Dianne Core, the national organizer of Childwatch, the charity monitoring abused children. Mrs. Core had come forward to provide conclusive corroboration of the worst that Dickens and Merry had been able to tell the man from *She*.

On a serious BBC documentary Audrey Harper admitted that she had taken part in human sacrifice in the context of black witchcraft. Williamson was on to her almost before she left the studio. 'It happened many years ago,' she said. 'Once, it was a baby girl, nine days old. She belonged to a woman in the coven. . . .' Williamson asked why no police prosecution had taken place. The answer was that it had taken the woman seventeen years to extricate herself from black witchcraft and that, in any event, she could not produce any evidence now.

In this respect the evidence Jane gave to *The Observer* was more valuable. Before extricating herself from the coven Jane had had a baby. The child had been removed from her by the coven and she had not seen it since. Her second child had been adopted for her own safety. It had been for the protection of her daughter that Jane had found the courage to make the final break.

Kevin Logan, vicar of St. John's, Blackburn, who had ministered to Greta in her final hours (see chapter 1) now came forward with evidence — photographic in some instances — to back up the testimonies and allegations which some appeared to be all too eager to dismiss as 'imagination gone wild'. 'You must realize', insisted Logan, 'that there is a tremendous resistance against materialism in our scientific age. People will always look for positive guidance, but if our churches are dead or full of ineffectual preachers then the Satanists have the strongest possible lead and, of course, they've made their appeal both forbidding and exciting. . . .'

Inside a coven. Williamson was able to observe and even infiltrate Satanist temples and witches' covens — but for a short time. Soon he, like MP Geoffrey Dickens, was receiving death threats. Those attracted to Satanism, he discovered, were often weak people manipulated by stronger people to the point where they had no longer been able to recognize the difference between good and evil and had become capable of anything. 'Satanists', Williamson wrote, 'cover a wide social spectrum: the rich mixed with the poor, the stockbrokers with the UB40s.'

In some instances initial contact with the occult had come via involvement with heavy metal music. Geoffrey Dickens reports: 'I hear more and more complaints of occult messages being slipped into heavy metal records. Rock groups vie with one another to flaunt their fascination with Satanism. Don't forget these groups have a huge following among impressionable youngsters. Exactly the age the Satanists seek.'

Satanism and rock. *Time* magazine has established a connection between 'heavy metal' music and Satanism. Their investigations began after a spate of suicides in Lethbridge, Alberta, had been linked with 'heavy metal' and Satanism. The suicides had been part of a group who had met at the home of a social worker where they had played music, taken drugs and dabbled in occult practices.

The Lethbridge story had come to the attention of the

Cardinal of New York, John O'Connor. According to *Time* the Cardinal had predicted that heavy metal music would lead to further suicides and had condemned it as 'pornography in sound'. In particular the Cardinal had denounced rocker Ozzy Osbourne's 'Suicide Solution'. Osbourne is believed by the Cardinal to be closely associated with the Satanism movement sweeping the USA.

The practice of Satanism had become widespread in the USA, reported the *Time* feature, even as Satan was losing currency in the seminaries. While the liberal theologians were doing their best to scratch Old Scratch, 'on the ground' churchmen were increasingly running up against occult practices. Father Richard Renton of Clifton, New Jersey, was cited as an example of a cleric who had sought to tackle the problem of Satanism. He had first become concerned when a 15-year-old in his parish had attempted suicide, saying that he wanted to meet Satan. 'It has become my work', says Renton, 'to inform parents and children that Satanism is not a lark. . . . Even the American Family Association has stated that it is beyond question that some rock music exploits Satanic and occult themes.'

Satanism in stockbroker belt. Back in the Thames valley Williamson had, by now, got himself an invite to a coven. It was, he discovered, a darkened room lit only by flickering candles; 'Dressed in black, with hooded robes, they wait expectantly for the Chief Satanist to begin the ceremony.

'They chant and call out to the Mighty One. The altar in the sparsely-furnished room is draped in a dark cloth and aloft there is the traditional pentagram. Some of the worshippers have already taken drugs, others have no need. A live cockerel is offered as a sacrifice. There is a great deal of sexual allusion contained in these rituals.' No actual child abuse took place while Williamson was present.

Geoffrey Dickens, MP for Saddleworth, has assembled a significant number of first-hand testimonies of the activities of what he describes as 'closed orders of Satanism' in which child abuse — and, he implies, child slaughter — has taken place. Dianne Core of Childwatch backs him up, pointing out that 'since black witches and Satanists, by the very nature of their pursuits lead highly-illegal lives, they are extremely meticulous about covering their tracks. . . . Children are being viciously abused in witchcraft ceremonies all over Britain. Flushed out of America, a great many paedophiles have now joined covens in my area (Humberside and the North-East) because they offer an easy way to gain access to children for sexual purposes. We have been gathering evidence of dreadful abuse and shocking initiation ceremonies in my part of the country. . . .'

Williamson and Dianne Core interviewed, together, a woman who had been a black witch from the age of 17. She told them, 'They draw their power from the devil. During my time as a black witch I saw and did things that I shall never be able to forget. The coven I joined initially got me when I was heavily hooked on drugs. They supplied my heroin free so, of course, I could never have backed out even had I wanted to. . . .'

Child abuse escalates by the year. Fifty-four thousand three hundred and fifty cases reported last year; an increase of 13 per cent on the previous year.

A mountain of evidence with regard to the paedophilia-satanist connection has been presented to the House of Commons by Geoffrey Dickens. The cries of thousands of abused children are being stifled. Is it possible that we owe it to ourselves and these children to expose the abuse — and uncover the power that drives the abusers?

CHAPTER SEVEN

ANNA, PACHITA AND VELVET CLAWS

'Just the sort of thing you need, Johanna. Lift you out of that black depression you've been in since university. Listen to this. . . .'

Johanna Michaelsen's father read the advertisement from the newspaper. It was the sort of thing she might have expected to read in California, or even Carolina, but here, out here in Cuernavaca, in small-town Mexico, it was so unusual it almost *had* to be taken seriously.

'The Mind Control Method. In forty-eight hours you can learn to use your mind to do everything you wish. You can learn to overcome depression, relieve insomnia, avoid irrational fears, develop ESP, and even gain peace of mind!'

Three days on, with a group of others of assorted ages, Johanna was reporting in for her first Mind Control session. A confident young man in his mid-thirties intoned, 'The aim is to function at your Alpha brainwave, that level of mind tapped by the great geniuses, the great artists and masters, the great psychics. . . . Deep relaxation and meditation occurs at this level. . . .'

There was, it appeared, *nothing* a 'controlled mind' could not do. All that was needed to speed up the mental and physical evolution of man was this forty-eight-hour training programme. . . .

Johanna entered it enthusiastically.

The last few years had been hell-above-ground. By the time she had left the University of North Carolina she was being ostracized by everyone (almost) because of her evident psychic powers. It had been the same during her years at Wesleyan College, Macon, Georgia. They had called her a witch. The seemingly unbreakable thread throughout: bouts of deep depression from which there seemed to be no escape.

It had all begun three months short of Johanna's twelfth birthday. Or, to begin at the *very* beginning, three years before that!

A prominent lay member of his local church, Johanna's father had hosted a visit from Bishop Pike and his family in 1963. Johanna had been fascinated by Jim Pike who seemed, in some sense, a kindred spirit. Then, in 1966, she had read of his drug-related suicide and, even more remarkably, of the psychic phenomena in his father's home that followed his death. That was, she writes in her book *The Beautiful Side of Evil* (Harvest House) 'the turning point of my life'.

Johanna had begun reading every available book on the occult; 'The deeper I studied the more aware I became of the spirits' almost tangible companionship. . . . I saw dark figures by my bed, heard soft voices calling to me.'

Before her thirteenth birthday, the house empty but for her sleeping baby sister and no sound but those of the quiet, Mexican summer night outside, she had heard doors banging of their own accord, bloodless feet treading stairs, and voices groaning. A spirit, she believed, had 'moved in' to the house.

When apparitions began to appear in the daytime, and the word got out in the community, it became impossible to employ domestic help.

'You must have inherited all this from your great aunt Dixie Jarratt,' said Johanna's mother reflectively. 'In her day she was acclaimed by the crowned heads of Europe. Even interviewed by Queen Victoria. . . .'

In her early days at Macon, Johanna had enjoyed a certain kudos because of what she had begun to see as her 'psychic potential'. For a time she had certainly given the powers of the unseen world the come-on.

Alone in the auditorium and working on a theatre production late one night she was suddenly aware of a dramatic temperature drop. Quite unmistakably a voice had spoken the words, 'This is *my* time — GET OUT!' At the time she had fled from the apparition in the long white dress. But subsequently the thought of it had preoccupied her. Sometimes on her own, occasionally with one or two others in the college theatre (and always at night) a presence had been sensed, and footsteps and a hysterical laugh heard. She had ended up by appeasing the phantom by offering it bouquets of flowers. . . .

To encourage her with a term paper on 'Voodooism in Haiti' an aunt had given her a ouija board. Friends had joined her in a dimly-lit room. The marker had begun to spell out messages. It had all seemed amusing and quite innocent — until one evening 'the presence that arrived was overwhelming in its feeling of evil'. This plus the ugly predictions made by the board concerning one of the girls, convinced Johanna that it was no innocent toy.

She had ended up a loner, the focus of frightened stares and glances.

Johanna pursued her enthusiasm for drama at the University of North Carolina. Here again a weird series of events had taken place in the theatre — and late at night. She had called the presence 'Professor Koch' after the founder of the drama school. For a time she had made a point of late-night visits to the theatre and of communicating with 'the professor'. Until, that is, the professor's mood turned ugly, and 'an overpowering presence of evil flooded into the theatre'.

Always there was depression, for long periods unrelieved.

Willing to try anything once, Johanna had begun to read the Bible. 'Reading the New Testament seemed to precede an especially violent and frightening attack from the beings around me, so I began to avoid it. . . .'

When she left university for her home town, forty-five miles north of Mexico City, black depression and fears of insanity enveloped Johanna.

Now she was sure that 'Mind Control' was the answer.

First, she had to learn relaxation techniques. Taped sounds of a metronome clicking monotonously, providing a soothing background. 'I took a deep breath and relaxed. . . .'

Within forty-eight hours Johanna was sure that it *was* possible to gain control over unknown forces and rise to the Alpha dimension.

She decided to continue the course.

On the third day she began to learn how 'to use visualization and image creation' to help 'develop intuition and subjective communication'.

A special laboratory was created for each student. Some time was taken to build them up. When Johanna's was complete she was told that she was ready to receive her 'counsellors'. Who would she choose? It could be anyone from Buddha to Grandma Moses!

After some thought Johanna decided to have as her counsellors Sarah Bernhardt — and Jesus Christ.

'We were counted slowly down to our Alpha level and entered our now fully-established laboratory. . . .' The room was filled with radiant light. A figure emerged. Brown hair, high forehead, brown eyes, olive skin. . . . For a second Johanna believed she had glimpsed the figure of Jesus.

After that Sarah Bernhardt was an anticlimax.

Later, at home, she was to wonder if she had imagined the whole thing.

So Johanna returned to her laboratory. On her own, without supervision, she began to count down to 'Alpha'. The crystals shone. She prayed that her counsellor 'Jesus' would appear. There was the same radiance, but something was amiss. The hair was wild and matted, the forehead covered with coarse fur — and the eyes gleamed with evil. The figure snarled and growled like an animal. She had thought she had seen the last of hell's terrors, and howled, 'Oh God — let me out!'

She decided that somehow she must have broken the rules.

At her next Mind Control session she asked to see 'Jesus' again. Again he appeared with werewolf characteristics.

But, when she found the courage to speak to him, he smiled gently and a beautiful human face appeared behind the hair.

At this stage, as far as Johanna was concerned, Mind Control had been a great success. At the suggestion of one of the organizers she made a trip into Mexico City. She was to meet Pachita. She had, they told her, shown great promise and was to experience a rare privilege.

The trip to Mexico City was made at night. Pachita lived in the back streets. Behind iron gates there was a narrow courtyard. To Johanna's surprise it was crowded with all kinds of people, rich and poor, Mexicans and Americans. She learned that Pachita was a great healer. Credence was added to this assertion by the presence of Dr. Carlos, a surgeon with his own practice in the area, who acted as one of Pachita's assistants.

Johanna entered, first, a small waiting room. It was very dark and heavy with the smell of dead roses and raw alcohol. Then came the 'operating room'. It had cement walls. A single light bulb hung from the ceiling. There was a small wooden table cluttered with rolls of cotton wool and bottles of alcohol. At one end there was an altar. Upon it were a number of candles, a picture of Christ on the cross and — central to the rest — a bronze statue of Cuauhtemoc, an Aztec prince who had borne torture and death at the hands of the Spaniards. At its feet lay a pair of surgical scissors and a rusty hunting knife.

Pachita herself was a tired old woman who gave every appearance of having had a stroke. Her hands were covered to the wrists with dry, crusted blood. Johanna was told to touch the Aztec statue three times.

After six days of 'spiritual and mental preparation' Johanna was to return to begin her 'life's work', she was told. She was to be an assistant to *Hermanito Cuauhtemoc*, the spirit that occupied Pachita during the healing operations.

On Friday 27 July 1971, in the company of Padre Humberto, a Catholic priest, Johanna presented herself at Pachita's house in Mexico City.

The courtyard and waiting room were full.

An 'operation' was already in progress. 'Powerful vibrations' emanated from the altar room, writes Johanna Michaelsen.

Before entering she was told: 'Be sure you remember not to address him as "Pachita". *It* is in her body, you will see, but *she* is not in it.'

Peering in, Johanna realized that Pachita was 'possessed'; her eyes were tight shut, there were no signs that she was in any sense 'present'. Hermanito was in full possession of her body.

In a voice far deeper than Pachita's own he commanded, 'To work, my daughter.'

Johanna was to assist Hermanito in many 'operations' over the next months and years.

Hermanito was, it appeared, known far and near as 'the great healer'.

One night, when rain hammered on the roof of the altar room, Hermanito operated on a woman called Rita for a cataract. The light bulb was switched off. A single candle on the altar was lit. A scrawny woman, always at Hermanito's side, carried protective 'holy balsam'. A chanting prayer commenced. Pachita's hands were rubbed in the balsam. Her eyes were closed. The atmosphere of the room thickened as a powerful, unseen presence descended upon her and Pachita became Hermanito.

Rita was ordered to sit in a chair. At Hermanito's direction large strips of cotton wool were cut and drenched with alcohol. Johanna's role, at Hermanito's behest, was to hold a large roll of cotton wool underneath Rita's chin.

Hermanito poured alcohol directly into Rita's eye. He then sprinkled balsam. Johanna, at his direction, handed him smaller cotton strips. He formed a square, leaving the eye exposed in the centre. Using scissors and the old hunting knife that lay on the altar — and to the background of an ancient Aztec prayer — Hermanito began to cut away the cataract. Rita was conscious throughout but professed to feel no pain.

When Hermanito had finished, the eye was bandaged. Rita was given red herb tea to drink. After three days the bandage was removed and it was found that the cataract had completely disappeared.

Johanna was convinced that she was doing 'God's work', as was her father. In the operation room, full of spirits, Johanna often saw the translucent, shimmering glow of her own counsellor 'Jesus' outshining the rest. . . .

In one of the more remarkable 'operations' at which she assisted, Johanna was handed a bottle of alcohol and a jar containing two vertebrae. One of the helpers explained, 'My friend in the morgue got these for me this morning — a poor man was run over last night.' This time Hermanito was operating on a 72-year-old man who had flown in from Los Angeles. First, Hermanito ascertained where exactly the back pain was located. The man was then placed on a plastic sheet on the floor. With the assistance of a pair of scissors, rolls of cotton wool soaked in alcohol or balsam and the vicious hunting knife, Hermanito proceeded.

Johanna's role was to keep the patient talking; 'I don't want him to lose consciousness,' said Hermanito.

Alcohol-soaked cotton wool was rubbed briskly over the old man's back. Four large pieces of dry cotton wool were arranged in a square, leaving the affected portion of the spinal column uncovered.

Hermanito plunged one end of the scissors into the back of the patient. Johanna saw the scissors disappear into the back, heard the flesh being cut and felt thick warm liquid flow into the cotton.

Hermanito took the knife, raised it in supplication, and then pushed it into the patient's back. Again there was a fresh surge of warm liquid. Hermanito hacked away for some considerable time before pulling out what seemed to be like a misshaped bone covered with blood. Hermanito announced that it was the damaged vertebra.

Operating through Pachita's body — with her tight-shut eyes — Hermanito took one of the vertebrae removed from the dead man in the morgue. With Pachita's bare hands he shoved it into the cavity from which the other bone had been removed. At that instant the whole room was filled with the foulest stench. Johanna's instinct was to throw up, but Hermanito ordered her to assist him as he removed a tumour that remained on the man's spinal column. 'He cut something loose just above my fingers and pulled out a round, stringy mass of flesh about the size of a golf ball which he then wrapped in cotton wool to be disposed of,' wrote Johanna.

Before the end of the operation the second vertebra taken from the dead man was inserted into the patient.

Then Hermanito announced he was leaving.

Both of Johanna's parents, as well as Padre Humberto, were among the witnesses of this operation.

It was Johanna's task to nurse the patient during his convalescence. He was to make a total recovery.

When the ordeal was over Johanna was to ask herself: Had it been sleight of hand or a fraud? Had she been hypnotized? The replacement of the vertebrae was medically impossible. She reflected, 'But my face was only inches from the wound. I myself had placed the strips of cotton wool I had cut on his skin. No one else had handled them. And I had a clear view of Pachita's hands, which were open, fingers spread. Nothing was palmed in them. At no time did she pull anything out from under her tunic; the dress she wore had no pockets anyhow. And I had felt the warm blood pulse over my hand. My hands were *in* the wound — blood was smeared to my wrists from it. But what she did was impossible!'

By now Johanna's parents were convinced believers.

As time went on she herself oscillated between the belief that it was 'God's work', and that 'the spiritists are right' and 'Hermanito' was the spirit of a dead man.

From time to time the authorities took an interest in the happenings at Pachita's house. She was even charged with practising medicine without a licence!

On some nights Johanna would assist as Hermanito

operated as many as six or seven times. Dramatic healings took place in this most unlikely — and most unhygienic — of 'operation rooms'. Always, apparently, with the same unsterilized 'surgical instruments', the scissors and the old hunting knife.

There *were* failures. Some immediate, and some in the longer term. But there were many outstanding successes.

By September 1972 Johanna had been working with Hermanito for fourteen months and been involved in approximately 200 operations. These operations had dealt with anything from broken limbs through slipped discs to brain tumours. She learned from Pachita that she had begun as a 'full-trance' medium and that this is how she had come to be possessed by Hermanito. She had been what he called his 'flesh' for forty-six years now.

Hermanito from time to time gave thanks to his 'father'. He also invoked 'God'. Were his methods God's methods? Or was he conscious that he was performing in a Roman Catholic country to a Roman Catholic 'gallery' — and wanted to mask his true identity?

Some of those upon whom Hermanito operated felt no pain. Others, says Johanna, suffered insupportable agony. In this, and in other respects, was Hermanito's healing method in any way reminiscent of that of Jesus Christ described in the four gospels?

And the appearances of 'Jesus' in Mind Control and in the operation room; Could these have been faked? Was a supernatural impersonator involved?

CHAPTER EIGHT

SPIRIT GUIDES AND SUPERSTARS

Shirley Maclaine was every well-calculated ounce the professional actress.

She demanded her scripts months before rehearsals began. Before she acted a scene or sang a song she wanted to be word and note perfect. Nothing was left to chance. Every moment had to be carefully choreographed.

And yet, here she stood on a bare stage fronting an audience of fifteen hundred. It included people from every conceivable occupation; scientists and home-makers, psychiatrists and megabuck tycoons, even the odd politician. Over that special weekend she knew she would occupy the stage alone for in excess of eighteen hours. And a 'compelling voice within' was urging her to abandon her meagre twenty-four-page script. . . . 'I had nothing to present but myself, the knowledge I had gleaned over the years, and my thoughts on esoteric, far-out concepts, based on strong personal experience.'

Ms. Maclaine took a deep breath and stood waiting. She made every attempt to empty her mind, make it 'vacant possession'.

The great ballroom was still.

Eyes wide open, Shirley silently appealed for help from the 'unseen dimension' populated by spirit guides for which she was America's best-known channeller (medium).

Power flowed into her; body and mind were in harmony, possessed. All sense of time was lost. 'An energy' filled the room. Everyone felt it. The 'sensitives' saw it. People grown weary of conventional religion, messiahs and gurus, were 'tapping into their internal power to elevate their lives to a higher octave of happiness and productivity'. A 'universal Divine Energy . . . a cosmic triad' took over speaker and, as minds were rendered vacuous through meditation techniques, listeners alike.

'All the time', writes Ms. Maclaine in *Going Within* (Bantam Books), 'I felt that my father was with me, helping me from the other side. . . .' Her long-dead father, she believed, was providing her scintillating thoughts and fluent outflow of words.

This 'seminar' — in Virginia Beach — was the first of a series, and the series one of a number by which a new movement swept America, a new movement of which Shirley was a high priestess.

What had begun for Shirley with the manifestation of a spirit guide who had told her of an *illicit amour* she was having with a married man (of which no one knew apart from the two participants) had drawn her into the vanguard of a vast though formless movement. This movement represented an amalgam of gnosticism, elements of Eastern religions, spiritualism and Satanism. Its keynote was the New Age. It touched (and took over) millions of lives from beatniks to peaceniks, from feminists to ecologists, from bankers to physicists, blue-, white-, and even no-collar workers. A movement so disparate as to defy analysis, but which would infiltrate the very bastions of orthodox Christianity and shake it at its foundations.

Among the millions touched and taken over was Will Baron.

Baron had been brought up in a Christian home in Manchester. His involvement began when he sought relief from a bowel ailment by joining a London-based organization called Health for the New Age. Soon he found himself moving to Los Angeles. He became a board member of a Theosophy-orientated New Age centre. For twelve years he worked as a New Age priest.

In the manuscript on which his book *Deceived by the New Age* (Pacific Press) is based, Baron indicates that his initial commitment was to a movement representing a reaction to conventional Christianity. A 60-year-old blond called Muriel ran the 'Lighted Way' sessions. She was a typical channeller (medium) of the New Age. In the course of seance-like sessions, deep male voices spoke through Muriel. The object of the sessions was to introduce others to channelling.

Will Baron proved an apt student. Soon a 'spirit' called Djwhal Khul came, not only to speak through him but, effectively, to control his life. If he showed resistance to the will of Djwhal Khul he would find himself subjected to terrifying ordeals by night followed by suicidal depression. This would only end when he bent his will to that of Djwhal Khul.

Will was told that the controlling spirits were 'christs', beings who, in the evolutionary process, had attained to a higher plain of existence than man. Will was at first disquieted when Muriel began speaking of Jesus Christ as, in some sense, superior to the other christs, and recommending her group to undertake Bible study. To Will this smacked too much of conventional Christianity. He felt he had risen above that. All avenues of religious expression, he had been taught, would ultimately lead to God, whether those expressions were coloured by Hinduism, Buddhism or anything else. Knowledge, success, and oneness with 'God' were the promises of the New Age Movement; and they sounded more sophisticated somehow than the 'forgiveness', 'salvation', 'abundant life' and 'everlasting life' promised by the Christian religion. At grammar school in England his teachers had exposed him to the theories of evolution, reincarnation and extrasensory perception. Ever since, Will had felt that Christianity was outmoded.

But here was Muriel recommending it in the strongest terms and announcing that, from here on, what had been known as the 'Lighted Way' sessions would be given over to Bible study. It was with some reluctance that Will Baron destroyed his impressive library of occult, metaphysical books. For reasons beyond his grasp at that stage Will was being drawn out of the Shirley Maclaine New Age Movement with its thinly disguised antipathy to Christianity.

Always a mixture of ideas, the New Age cauldron for Will was now receiving a hefty dose of Christian ideas and jargon. How would this affect his relationship with Djwhal Khul? he wondered. Had not the great 'master' actually rewarded him with a personal manifestation after he had taken his vow of celibacy? He found it difficult to forget that 'shining person radiating intense golden-white light that almost blinds you by its brilliance' that had been Djwhal Khul in person. Or the crisp, clear, spirit voices that regularly spoke to him during the hours of meditation in his flat.

Why would 'the masters' want him to study the Bible, attend Christian congregations and, to all intents and purposes, appear like a conventional Christian? Muriel insisted that that was what was required of Baron. She also claimed to be able to channel 'the Father' and that Baron's change of direction was 'the Father's will'. Channellings were cloaked in King James version language now. There was even biblical exposition of a sort. Muriel claimed that the tall, commanding presence of Jesus Christ appeared to her in a hotel bedroom and ordered her to 'Get down on your knees'! This impressed her; she went so far as to instruct her followers to pray 'in the name of Jesus'.

In the context of Muriel's classes, using a TV set, a careful study was made of the techniques of the TV evangelists. Muriel was at pains to point out how much the evangelists were influenced by New Age teaching. Attending a 6,000-strong convention addressed by one of them, Baron had an opportunity to test the accuracy of Muriel's observations. In the early meetings he heard only conventional Bible-based preaching. Only at the later meetings did he realize that the evangelist was, in fact, regularly employing New Age jargon and expounding New Age concepts. At the final meeting he almost fell off the edge of his seat; the evangelist made the same striking prediction that Muriel had made a short time before. Jesus, he said, accompanied by His angels, would soon begin to appear in a physical form in the churches and would be seen walking down the aisles, and would then disappear. . . .

Baron was in for another shock.

At Muriel's next Bible study she announced, 'Jesus told me that Djwhal Khul has fallen.' This went against all previous teaching. Grinning, she continued, 'I think Djwhal Khul may be Satan.'

'Jesus' now began to channel through Muriel. Through her he told the group that the Lighted Way was now to be considered a Christian church.

Baron was confused.

Gradually he convinced himself that 'Jesus' was calling him to his fold. He attended the Sunday services of a variety of Christian denominations. It does not appear to have perturbed him that 'Jesus' channelled through Muriel in exactly the same way as the dead 'masters' had, the implicit assumption being that he too was dead and required a medium through whom to speak.

One night Baron was genuinely scared when his bed shook, fixtures and fittings swayed. The audible voice of 'Jesus' spoke with greater power than Djwhal Khul had ever done (though the message was no more than that it was time he took up jogging!). Soon be became accustomed to the voices and manifestations of 'Jesus'.

He found he did not miss Djwhal Khul. The supernatural phenomena that gatecrashed his life had not changed. All that had changed was that, having acquired a working knowledge of the Bible, he had become part of several Christian congregations and was busily introducing them to New Age beliefs — in effect a counterfeit Christianity — up front being the tenet that soon Jesus Christ could be expected to begin making personal appearances in certain congregations. . . .

Meanwhile, night after night, Will would wake to find that his whole house was shaking as if in an earthquake. His bed would shudder. Then he would hear the voice of 'Jesus' booming the words, 'I am coming soon. You have to do my work. Time is running out.'

In these night-time visitations impossible demands would be made on him by 'Jesus'.

When he would resist the demands, intense, insupportable depression invariably set in. Depression to the point where he would curse the name of Jesus Christ — and feel that the only way out was suicide.

'Jesus' was making Will Baron's life hell.

So who or what are the 'spirit guides' speaking through New Age channellers?

What or who are the 'masters' behind the infiltration of Christian congregations with well-briefed New Age 'phonies'? How much does the New Age have in common with Christianity? What possible motive could there be behind the New Age claim that Jesus Christ is soon to appear to selected congregations in a physical form? And exactly how much did the 'Jesus' of Will Baron's second New Age phase have in common with the New Testament's Jesus of Nazareth? And how much with Djwhal Khul and other 'spirit masters'? What conceivable motive could the spirit world of Shirley Maclaine's 'unseen dimension' have in producing a counterfeit Christ?

CHAPTER NINE

'THIS CAN'T BE THE END OF IT . . . '

The night gale had been furious.

At first light I peered out over the back garden. Sixty-five feet of six foot, latticed fencing had been converted into so much matchwood. Shrubs and rose bushes, leafless, had been flattened underneath it. A palaver of seabirds was surveying the damage. An equivalent number were strutting around in our neighbours' garden, of which we now had an unobstructed view.

Watery March sunlight encouraged me to venture outdoors to tend my worse-for-weather shrubs. It was then that I heard a gurgle, a grunt, and a crackle of infant laughter. On all fours, looking at me from the other side of where the fence had been was Carrie, displaying her broadest, most engaging grin. She was pointing at our old jack-rabbit skipping and cavorting around. In the certain knowledge it was all being done for her entertainment, Carrie was in raptures.

Soon, folding one leg under, she was propelling herself with two plump arms and the other leg, to fetch Mum and Dad.

Until that day Carrie had been only a noise through the wall. And her mum and dad, in their mid-twenties, had not even been that. In the months that followed we found that that furious night-time gale had found us a gold mine of friendship.

From now on the first pleasurable sensation on each of my mornings was to see Carrie, nappy-lagged, with one hand on the chain-link, the other pointing as, in a burst of scribble-talk, she demanded that the jack-rabbit be let out of its night quarters for her amusement.

As spring became summer Carrie was growing fast. Soon she could walk. At first, in a staggering, drunken sort of way. But for her chuckling disposition, you might even have said she was a little bruiser.

I never saw such delighted parents. Linda was the proudest mother for miles. Out shopping, the butcher, the baker and the fish-and-chip maker all had a word for Carrie. John, six-and-a-half feet tall, with breadth to match, member of the local cricket club, could scarcely contain himself. Whenever he was at home he could be heard chortling, making baby noises, for the benefit of his little tomboy.

Carrie was full of character, life, energy and mischief. When she went to bed of an evening she left behind a trail of wreckage — the lawn still bestrewn with her building blocks, her horse and her wheelbarrow, her mother collapsed in a chair. Needless to say, that fence never got rebuilt.

Autumn came late that year. Warm weather lasted well into November, and Carrie's laughter could still be heard through our open windows.

But one day it stopped.

That Wednesday it was already dark when I arrived home. No one was in at Carrie's house. There were toys in the garden but no light in the house or car in the drive. In the small hours of Wednesday morning I had heard the sounds of activity, and the revving of a car engine, but had gone back to sleep and had not called it to mind in the morning.

When I arrived home on Wednesday evening they told me that something terrible had happened next door. We should not hear the sound of Carrie's laughter again.

On Tuesday Carrie had developed a cough. Her mother rang the doctor but the receptionist said there could be no appointment before Thursday. Carrie was taken to the doctors anyway and she was 'fitted in'. The doctor said there was no cause for alarm and that Carrie should be kept indoors. At 2am on Wednesday morning she had been taken to the hospital because she was finding difficulty in breathing. A few hours after being admitted she died. On Friday the coroner pronounced, 'Bronchial pneumonia'.

We were unstrung for weeks. And there is no word adequately to describe the feelings of Linda and John. John was terribly bitter at the incompetence of medicine men . . . but there was more, much more. Linda alternated between being flaccid, and another more extrovert emotion that bordered on hysteria . . . but there was more, much more.

Six days after Carrie's death I arrived early for her funeral and, in another furious gale, with three representatives of the cricket club, waited for the arrival of the mourners and the tiny coffin. The minister — young chap, evangelical Anglican — spoke of the attitude of Jesus towards little children. . . . Said that Carrie was assured of a place in God's kingdom and that we could only have the same assurance in so far as we were like her. As we huddled around the grave his words were blown away by the wind . . . dust to dust, ashes to ashes. . . .

We all felt terribly empty, like the vacuum in life that Carrie left behind. . . . Her clothes, her toys, collected up and given away. . . . On her grave in the wind-blown cemetery was a large wreath in the shape of a rabbit, 'To Carrie With Love. What shall we do without you? Mum and Dad.' The bitter, furious wind blew sharp particles of leaf and frost into our sensitized faces and, howling, expressed our outrage. Why? Why? Why?

John fixed the minister with fierce, angry eyes and demanded: 'This *can't* be the end of it . . . ?'

Well, can it?

When death strikes we are pulled up with a jolt. We are conscious there is a void in our lives; that there are questions in our minds for which we have never received convincing answers. And we ask ourselves, Is death 'the final curtain'? If so, what is the meaning of life? Is there any foundation for the idea ingrained in popular theology of 'man's immortal soul'? Is there life after life? If so, what form does it take?

Each of us demands, 'This *can't* be the end of it!' Suddenly we realize that the fear of death is not the sharpest anxiety born of our mortality: the deeper fear is that life has no meaning and must end in ultimate extinction — that oblivion will crown the toil and sacrifice of successive generations.

What is at stake when we exclaim, 'This *can't* be the end of it . . . !'? It's not just comfort for the bereaved. It is the validity of man's belief in right and wrong. It is the significance of his decisions. It is the underwriting of all man's high endeavour and spiritual travail as eternally worth while. If death is indeed 'the final curtain', the end of everything, then life is devalued, and man no more than self-deluded, animated dust.

Even those who claim to have outgrown a belief in life after life still pore over the artefacts of past ages and hear the rustle of time's turning leaves, and seek themselves to leave behind something that will outlive them, that time cannot destroy. They are aware of their impermanence. They long for immortality. They too, in their own way, are saying, 'This *can't* be the end of it!'

When John first said that, perhaps what he meant by it was: Why did Carrie have to be born, show such promise, then die, suddenly, the dawn of her fulfilment still on the rim of the eastern horizon?

But as the days went by — and then the weeks, and now the years — John's question broadened, but it lost none of its urgency.

He felt compelled to find an answer to it.

Why are we *all* born, show promise, work at the daily grind, surround ourselves with roof, supports and 'consumables' — and then die, our memory soon to be lost in the sea of forgetfulness?

John would thrust his questions, without notice, in front of anyone. He got right back to basics. . . .

What are we? Where did we come from? Is man no more than a chance arrangement of protons and electrons which, after eons of time, evolved into an upright creature with two

legs and a brain? Did it really all start with a primeval
mollusc crawling out of some swamp? Did life result from
a biological accident?

This was the low-down they had given him at school, he
told me. The life cycle, they had reckoned, got under
starter's orders when the ancestral mollusc oozed out of that
swamp. That much he'd picked up in Biology. After considering its needs for a while — call it a couple of million
years to be on the safe side — it had, apparently, developed
into something slightly more ambitious than a snail. It had
grown arms, legs and other appropriate appurtenances — all
in easy stages.

After mutating, adapting, and propagating at the expense
of other species, it had grown the beginnings of a fist.
Allowing plenty of time, one day it had taken its first
arthritic stride. And the story, begun in the biology class,
was continued in the history class. . . .

Bows and arrows, swords and spears, cannons and
muskets, Molotov cocktails, bombs, A-bombs, H-bombs and
intercontinental ballistic missiles. . . . Peasant insurrections,
reigns of terror, six-day wars, hundred-year wars, world
wars, Robespierre, Hitler and Saddam Hussein. . . .

Industrial effluent, carbon monoxide, strontium 90, earth
warming and the erosion of the ozone layer. . . .

An over-populated planet with six billion inhabitants, two-
thirds without enough to eat . . . each individual, one six-
billionth of the total, about as important as a grain of sand
on the seashore . . . no purpose, no life-meaning . . . the
affluent getting by on alcohol, nerve pills and, of an evening,
helpings of fantasy dished up courtesy of TV and video. . . .

'You know,' John told me one day, 'if that's all there is
to it, I've got to get alongside any ambitious, swamp-
dwelling mollusc and tell him to *stay put*. If that's all there
is to it, Carrie is best out of it. . . . But, it *can't* be. All
there is to it, that is. *Can* it?'

The greatest danger that faces man is not death itself, but
the belief that life's origin was accidental, and, therefore,

that 'being has no meaning' and will end in ultimate extinction, man's toils and strivings crowned with oblivion. The effects of this belief — fear, confusion, superstition, despair, scepticism towards the future and cynicism towards men — are not a sustainable diet for the human spirit. It is *possible* to drag out a dull existence beclouded by these feelings, but without faith it is *impossible* to live nobly, profitably, enjoyably, hopefully.

And that is what I told John. And I believe it. Faith is not the alternative to reason, it is a reasoned belief in the incredible. It is the alternative to self-depreciation and a pointless, aimless life. Nothing stymies fulfilment like the lack of faith. To lack it is to limit all human endeavour. To have it is to strive beyond the swamp of hopelessness through the door of infinite possibility and high adventure. In John and Linda's situation there was a choice between faith and faithlessness. And that choice implied another: between hope and hopelessness.

John talked with us for a long time. Not all of a sudden, but over time, both he and Linda found faith. And a foundation for faith in a personalized trust in God. They found God because they went in search of Him and, to their surprise, found He was looking for them. They found God revealed in a Book, the textual accuracy of which has been miraculously preserved down the arches of the centuries.

John and Linda came to know the God who chose to live in a veined, nerved, sinewed body like anyone else's, in a community like theirs, in the person of Jesus Christ. Through this Book and this Man their life now has purpose and direction.

Listen to John; 'I found that I was not an insect on a speck of stardust, or the result of a biological accident; I was made by God in His image and, though one of six billion, am important to Him. A force of evil exists in the world, and to save me from its fall-out and to enable me to live for ever in a better world, Jesus lived, died, and was resurrected.'

As time went on, John and Linda were to discover that the Bible's message did not end there. They discovered that a huge proportion of the New Testament is preoccupied with another theme. The fall-out of sin in the world was such, they discovered, that a new beginning is planned for. This new beginning, they found, would not just involve a re-creation of the physical world. It would involve a re-awakening of those who, like Carrie, had fallen into the sleep of death. ' "Dust to dust, ashes to ashes," that's what the parson said,' said John. 'But that's not the end of it. One day there will be a re-creation and a welcome to God's eternal day. And, as the parson said, we shall receive that welcome in so far as we've been, like Carrie, as little children living on trust and by the fuel that God provides — faith.'

A great thought, that.

It means that Carrie's story is not finished yet.

John and Linda and the rest of us will see that grin and hear the familiar crackle of infant laughter again. And this time Carrie's story will go on for ever. Not in some shadowy world of spirits at the beck and call of psychics but in the glorious brilliance of God's eternal Kingdom.

CHAPTER TEN

WHO ARE THE ALIENS?

So what *was* that alien force that reduced Les and his gang of mucho machos to jelly?

Who *is* picking up the psychic telephone and answering from 'the other side'?

Medium Brenda Crenshaw — who claims to know a thing or three about 'the other side' — warned that 'there are spirits . . . who are willing to come back to a medium and take possession of him'. So what or who *are* these spirits and where did they come from?

Veteran New Ager Ruth Montgomery warned that channelling was potentially 'opening a door through which mischievous and malevolent spirits might enter'. Today that 'door' is being opened in spiritist seances and New Age gatherings in all Western lands. Isn't it time that we identified the spirits and the source from whence they are coming?

What *is* the power behind the resurgence of Satanism and its apparent corollary, the sexual abuse of children?

It's all in the Book. The great questions of life, death, time and eternity are answered for the Christian in the Book of books, the Bible.

Against the longest odds imaginable the discovery of ancient manuscripts in the last 150 years or so has demonstrated that its text has not been corrupted by time. Over the same period the findings of archaeologists have authenticated as fact the details of its narrative previously contested or, in some instances, laughed off as mythical. (See the author's *The Battle for the Book*, Autumn House.)

The manuscript evidence for the New Testament alone is far in excess of that for any other document of antiquity. There are 5,300 Greek manuscripts, 10,000 Latin Vulgate manuscripts and more than 9,300 manuscripts of other early versions. The next most authenticated work is Homer's *Iliad* for which 643 manuscripts survive. Further to this, in no other case is the time interval between the original work and the earliest extant manuscript so brief as in the case of the New Testament. The John Ryland's Papyrus, a part of John's gospel, dates from circa AD 120, approximately twenty years after the original was written by John.

But the manuscripts and the artefacts are merely evidences for faith. The Bible is self-authenticating. It is the sort of book that a man could not write if he would, and would not write if he could. The content of the book is such that men and women, by exposing themselves to it, can discover that it is inspired by God.

Its readers find it to be as real as the blood pulsing through their arteries, as real as the earth beneath their feet. The adventure with God into which it leads brings the reader —

* *To his roots.* Matter plus Time plus Chance do *not* make a world. Man, matter and time exist by divine fiat. Man was made in the image of an all-powerful, all-knowing, all-loving Creator God. His roots are among eternal things.

* *To purposeful living.* The God who made man in His image loves him as an everlasting Father. Life *is* more than a dusty scuffle over a parched terrain between Point Birth and Point Death. Life *is* more than a catalogue of accidents. Life *is* more than a nightmare between two eternities. Life committed to God has purpose and aim, and both are tied up in a relationship of trust into which all comers are invited.

* *To ultimate security.* God's love is stronger than that of any parent. The God of the Bible gives no copper-bottomed guarantee that His children will not encounter problems and difficulties. What He *does* guarantee is that when the problems and difficulties come, He will walk by their side. That He hurts when they hurt. That no hurt will come their way until it has been sieved through His love, grace and power. That when it strikes — even though some of our questions may remain unanswered until we meet Him

face to face — it will be made to work in some way for our everlasting good.

＊ *To fear-free living.* God is Sovereign, all-powerful. The world is more like a ship than an iceberg. The iceberg cracks off from the polar ice-cap in a thunderous explosion. After that its course and destiny are subject to all kinds of uncertainties. A ship has a captain, a navigator, charts, maps, and navigational equipment. The God of the Bible is a Captain who says, 'Trust me regardless of the storms and I'll guide the vessel into an eternal harbour. Examine my record as set out in the Book. Look at the events foretold years before they happened and how they came to pass. See how I have set out my scenario of the future. Trust me in the little things of Time; I am concerned with the details of your life. Trust me in the big things of Eternity; I want to guide you through the worst to the ultimate best.'

＊ *To guilt-free living.* Neither the Bible nor the God revealed in its pages have any illusions about man. God made men and women perfect. On behalf of the rest of us, the first Adam gave in to the force of evil present on the planet. That force led man, with his consent, into depravity and corruption. The natural tendency of the human choice-mechanism is towards the worst, rather than the best. But the Bible tells us how, though eternal right must be maintained, eternal love found a way to save sinners through the second Adam, God's own Son. That God gives both sin-sorrow and forgiveness; both the impulse to desire the best (against man's own nature), and the new life that *is* the best (against man's own deserts).

＊ *To ultimate hope.* The Bible promises that a glorious new world — beyond the pain and injustice of the present — awaits those who enter the new life amid the sorrows and uncertainties of the now. This is its message. In an uncertain world the assurance of eternity is possible. In an evil-choked world forgiveness, acceptance and high-level living are possible. In a world of conflict it is possible to live with supernatural peace. In a world of heartbreak it is possible to have a joy of the sort that it is in no man's power to take from you.

God has opened the way through his Son, the second Adam. *Everything* is possible through trusting Him, and establishing a day-by-day relationship with Him. *That* is the message of the Bible.

The alien force. Most psychics believe that the spirits who speak through them in the darkened rooms are dead people. Some believe that the source is God. A few candidly warn that the unseen dimension is dangerous and potentially destructive. All accept that the genuineness of the spirit is determined by the nature of the information in its 'message'.

This is a dangerous assumption.

Medium Crenshaw is quite open about this. After a lifetime of mediumship she still believes that the accuracy of a particular message is no proof that it 'has come from a particular person named' — usually a deceased loved one. She invites us to entertain the possibility that it may come from 'another authority'.

A 'miracle' can be a fraud. That is not to say that mediums and channellers do not have a hot line to an unseen dimension. But we are suggesting that that unseen dimension has nothing to do with the dead and nothing to do with God. While psychics have always been disturbed by the tendency of the spirits to lie and give disinformation, they have continued — when accurate information with regard to a person's past or situation is given — to accept these accurate messages as acid proof that 'supernatural good' is involved. Is this where their logic breaks down? Is it possible that in the spirit world there are talented impersonators with access to unlimited information with regard to an individual's circumstances and past life? Who *are* the inhabitants of the unseen dimension, the spirit world?

Canon Michael Green was once 'invited to sign an open letter deploring the credulity of those who thought that demons still existed or were foolish to believe in a personal devil'. The Canon refused to sign. He gives his reasons in his book *I believe in Satan's Downfall* (Hodder and

Stoughton); 'It seemed to me that the *naïveté* might possibly lie with those who wished so summarily to dispose of His Infernal Eminence.' Modern Christians, believes Green, are right to jettison the horns-and-cloven-hooves devil. Such a picture is unscriptural. But, says Green, the Bible 'very seriously warns us of a malign power of evil standing behind the pressures of a godless world without and a fallen nature within the Christian'.

This is how Canon Green sees it. There is a devil whose aim is to rebel against God and embroil the whole cosmos in his rebellion. He is the enemy of man, but a defeated enemy — the death blow having been delivered by Christ at Calvary. Nevertheless he continues to be very active and is never more pleased when the idea of his existence is held in ridicule. He feels like a general who has persuaded the opposition to underestimate him. 'Doubt about the existence of a malign focus of evil is to be found,' writes Green, 'by and large, only in Christian lands.' Perhaps, if Satan were better known, he would be more hated, more resisted, and more defeated in the lives of Christians.

Canon Green links belief in a personal devil with belief in a personal God. 'By far the most reasonable assumption is that behind our intelligible and moral sphere there lies a supreme intelligence and will. The name we give to it is God. But as we reserve the variety of forms in which evil, no less than good, shows itself, are we not to suppose that there is an organizing spirit of supreme evil and malignity? The name we give to it is Satan.'

Because there is design in our world we accept a Designer. Facts support belief: the existence of moral qualities such as beauty, truth and goodness; the uniformity of nature which suggests a beneficent Creator and Sustainer. Do not similar considerations infer the existence of Satan? Are there no marks of design in the forces of evil which form so large a part of our daily news coverage? Does not the existence of wicked characteristics — the very opposite of beauty, truth and goodness — point beyond our world to an evil source of these things? Do not the escalating horrors of our world in themselves point in the same direction?

In every generation there are men who seem to be monsters, the very embodiment of evil. It is hard to believe of them that wickedness is merely the absence of good. Evil is a mighty force, flowing from men and women and afflicting all within their range. Is it so improbable that they are, in fact, the instruments of Satan, a supernatural centre and embodiment of evil who fouls all he touches?

That behind the evil in the world and in man there is an organizing genius, a focus of horror far greater than man himself?

Canon Green concludes his argument; 'In our own day and in our own country there are plenty of people worshipping Satan directly, and by the exercise of black magic are discovering the reality of spiritual forces to which they were previously complete strangers. . . . When men and women deliberately seek occult powers, they very quickly discover that these powers are both real and terrible. . . . Many get sucked in through playing with ouija boards, reading tarot cards, experimenting with levitation or going to seances. Charms and horoscopes have, to my certain knowledge, brought dangerous and damaging exposure to the reality of evil forces. . . . Anyone who has seen the astounding contrast between a person possessed by an occult force and that same person set free by Christ fully and completely — it may be only an hour later — will not need any persuading that man has a mighty, hateful enemy in Satan.'

As more and more churchmen are coming to believe: it's all in the Book.

From Genesis to Revelation we encounter an anti-god force of great power and cunning. He is arrogant and determined, the implacable foe of God and man, who is out to spoil and mar all that is good and lovely. We find him in the Garden of Eden at the beginning of the story. We find him in the lake of fire at the Bible's end.

Jesus believed in Satan and had more to say about him than anyone else in Scripture. Satan is the one who tempted

Him so skilfully and fiercely — as he tempts us — and who kept coming back at Him with devious suggestions all through His ministry. There could be no compromise with this evil force. Hence the cross. It sounded the death knell for the usurper. It was as He spoke of the cross that Jesus cried: 'Now shall the prince of this world be cast out. . . .' John 12:31.

On the last night of his life Jesus reiterated the reality of Satan, ' "The ruler of this world is coming. He has no power over me. . . ." ' John 14:30, RSV.

Where the aliens came from. This is the Bible picture.

Satan began as one of God's creatures. He was a spirit of great ability, who became consumed by pride, rebelled, lost his position and began a long struggle against the government of God. He was cast out of heaven with a third of the heavenly host (angels turned demons).

Revelation 12:7-9 recounts the origin of evil and the expulsion from heaven. Verse 4 infers that a third of the angelic host was expelled with Satan.

Scholars accept that Isaiah's tirade against the king of Babylon in chapter 14 of his book is really a tirade against another and more sinister figure than the literal king of Babylon. (See verses 12-14.) The Isaiah passage clarifies the issue which originated Satan's rebellion.

Ezekiel (chapters 26-28) provides more background. The first ten verses of chapter 28 speak of the *prince* of Tyre, while the next nine speak of the *king* of Tyre. In Ezekiel's day Tyre was a prosperous and luxurious island kingdom lying to the north-west of Israel. When Ezekiel directs his message to the *prince* of Tyre he uses language appropriate to a man. The language he directs to the *king* of Tyre is highly inappropriate to any man; it could not be used of any human being. Exactly the same spirit dominates the prince as the king. However, it is clear that when referring directly to the king, Ezekiel is speaking of Satan, and when referring to the prince he is referring to Satan's power and character demonstrated through a man. (See especially Ezekiel 28:12-17.)

Taken together the passages in Revelation 12, Isaiah 14 and Ezekiel 28 answer the question: Who inhabits the unseen dimension of the spirit world, where did they come from and how did their evil nature originate?

There was an inter-galactic war — heaven's top angel officer — next to the Son of God — brilliant — intelligent — beautiful — but proud. Proud enough to challenge the authority of God's government. Lucifer (Satan) and his followers were cast out of heaven — and earth became the theatre of war.

Jesus himself said (Luke 10:18, RSV) ' "I saw Satan fall like lightning from heaven." ' His words had an immediate application: seventy of His followers had returned triumphant, having cast out demons in His name. But His words represented also an historical statement. Jesus — the Christ who had existed from the beginning (John 1:1) — was recalling the great inter-galactic conflict back in the mists of pre-history and, in His mind's eye, recalling the fall of Satan and his hosts.

Church fathers like Tertullian believed that Jesus' words about Satan's fall from heaven were a direct allusion to Isaiah 14:12 and that Jude's reference (verse 6, RSV) to 'the angels that did not keep their own position but left their proper dwelling' was also to be understood against a background of God's expulsion of Satan and his hosts.

Who *are* the aliens who — when invited by occult dabblers — introduced the terrors of hell into homes and lives?

They are angels turned demons — intelligent, observant, who, whether seen or unseen, have infested this planet for the thousands of years since the cosmic conflict began.

Who *is* picking up the psychic telephone and answering from 'the other side'?

'They are the spirits of devils, working miracles.' Revelation 16:14. Mischievous spirits with access to information about past and present and who, because of their evil stratagems, are able to hazard shrewd guesses about some things that will happen in the future. Spirits whose activities have been whipped up into a fury because they are aware that their time is short.

' "Rejoice, O heavens! you citizens of heaven, rejoice — be glad! But woe to you people of the world, for the Devil has come down to you in great anger, knowing that he has little time." ' Revelation 12:12, Living Bible.

Back in 1848, in their home in Hydesville, New York, the Fox family had been troubled by mysterious rappings. There were two daughters, Katie, aged 12, and Margaretta, aged 15. One night young Katie sat up in bed and uttered the words, 'Mr. Splitfoot, do as I do.' Thereafter she found that 'Mr. Splitfoot' was a highly-intelligent, alien being. However, in naming him thus Katie displayed a shrewdness beyond her years. Her clear reference to the devil represented a psychic hole-in-one. Modern dabblers in the world of the occult would do well to heed the warning implicit in the young girl's form of address. . . .

But if the devil was defeated at Calvary, where are the limits of his power? Surely, he cannot *always* have it his own way . . . ?

CHAPTER ELEVEN

WHERE THE DEVIL CAN'T SEE

Helmut left Germany for the winter games in Finland.

Enjoying the thrills and spills of the vast amusement park connected with the games, Helmut made the acquaintance of a Finnish girl, Annele.

Neither Helmut nor Annele believed in God or knew anything about the Bible.

Close to midnight one evening they noticed a hut on the edge of the amusement park, set aside from the rest. It looked weird. They were curious.

Outside it said: 'Fortune Teller'.

They giggled, and went in.

Inside, they crossed the palm of a wizened old woman with silver. She told them their fortune; 'You will have many difficulties, but no power on earth will ever separate you. You will marry' — at this the couple smiled self-consciously; they weren't even fond of one another — 'after a year a son will be born. After another year a second son will be born.'

Suddenly the old woman was caught up in convulsions. She looked terrified and tried hard to speak but could not. Shaking violently and retching she stood up and blurted, screamed really: '*I cannot see further. . . .*'

Startled, Helmut and Annele ran out into the night.

The couple parted the following day. Helmut returned to Germany. They had no intention of seeing each other again, though they *did* exchange addresses. As the months went by they began to write to one another. Six months later Annele visited Helmut and his family in Germany. Despite many difficulties placed in their way they decided to marry.

A year later a son was born to them.

They gave up their small flat and rented a larger one in a building in Hamburg called Advent House. Every week a large number of people gathered in the church that occupied the ground floor of their 'house' and had a meeting. They appeared to be fond of one another and stood around for ages after the religious service had finished.

Annele became pregnant a second time. Fear gripped her heart with cold fingers. She remembered the fortune teller's prediction. So far her predictions had been fulfilled. What would happen now? The old woman had not been able to see past the birth of their second son. Would Annele die in childbirth? Would they both be killed in a terrible accident?

Helmut and Annele were in great anxiety night and day.

They had never done so before, but now they began to pray. And they began to read a book that the caretaker of Advent House had given them on the day they had moved in. Their attention became focused on eternal things.

Until now the Christians downstairs had been a joke. But, as they began to meet with them, their all-consuming anxiety began to evaporate.

Shortly after the birth of their second son Helmut and Annele gave their hearts to Jesus Christ and were baptized by immersion.

The baptism was, at once, a beginning and a symbol of a wonderful experience which had already taken place. They had been 'born again'. An old life for them had come to an end. A new life had begun. They had made a 180 degree turn. What was formerly ahead of them was now behind them. What was formerly behind them was now ahead of them. Good and evil had changed places. With their eyes on Jesus Christ they were walking in a completely new direction.

In this rite of baptism the death, burial and resurrection of the Lord Jesus Christ was symbolized. Paul the apostle referred to this symbolism in Romans 6: 'When we were baptized into union with Christ Jesus, we were baptized into union with his death. By our baptism, then, we were buried with him and shared his death, in order that, just as Christ was raised from death by the glorious power of the Father, so also we might live a new life. For since we have become one with him in dying as he did, in the same way we shall be one with him by being raised to life as he was. . . . Since we have died with Christ, we believe that we will also live with him.' (Verses 3-5, 8, Good News Bible.)

The apostle is explaining the symbolism of new birth. By identifying with the death of Jesus, we have accepted Him as our personal Saviour from sin, and our sins have been nailed to His cross.

By identifying with His burial our sins are buried with Him, forgotten as far as God is concerned.

We identify with the resurrection of Jesus by rising with Him to a new, far more meaningful life of joy, peace and assurance in which sin as a habit of life has been left behind; we are indwelt by the Holy Spirit and spend each day in the company of the risen Lord. In place of sin-slavery, by the power of God and our love response for salvation, positive virtues develop in our lives as spontaneously as grapes grow on a vine. The power of sin is on the wane.

The parallel symbolism of baptism and new birth was explained to Helmut and Annele by the pastor.

Following their baptism they told him their story.

He smiled.

Candidly he admitted that he could not explain completely how the fortune teller had been able to see so far into their future. He was sure the devil was in it somewhere. But the devil had not been able to reveal to the fortune teller what would happen after the birth of their second son. He had peered into their future and his fear had been expressed in the antics of the old woman; her scream had been his scream. The devil had not been able to reveal to her that our heavenly Father can begin a completely new life for us through a new birth.

'You *must* be born again,' said Jesus. Admit your need of God. Confess your sin-sorrow. Surrender your life to God. He is either Lord *of all*, or He is not Lord *at all*!

This is the message of the Gospel.

The teaching of Jesus meets the deepest cries and needs of men and women of all cultures, of all ages. He is the light in our darkness; the purpose in an otherwise purposeless life; the meaning in an otherwise meaningless existence.

We can enter a new life through a new birth. And it starts at the cross.

Christ is the central figure in Scripture.

The cross is its central symbol. All Scripture and (according to Scripture) all history lies beneath its shadow.

The very shape of the cross suggests the length, breadth and height of the love of God. It points to heaven from where Jesus came. It is rooted in the earth He came to redeem. The outstretched hands on the transverse beam are an invitation to all men — even to His crucifiers.

Men may reject an angry God. But how can they reject God who, even at the point of their rejection, leans forward in entreaty?

Sin and guilt are left at the cross. An old life can die there, and a new life be born. And that new life is the beginning of an everlasting adventure.

Every devil from wherever devils come from was present at Calvary. It was Satan's great chance to upset God's plan for the salvation of man.

But when Jesus died there was a cry of triumph on his lips: 'It is finished!' 'Mission accomplished!'

The salvation of man was accomplished. Jesus had died as a sacrifice; died with the sins of the whole world upon His shoulders. Died for every man and woman who has and will ever live. By accepting Jesus as their Saviour men can have forgiveness of sin and a new life.

That, above all, is why Calvary makes the devil tremble.

It was the central battle of the age-long conflict between good and evil. And the battle was won: by good and by God. Man was given freedom to choose *not* to be evil. And the devil's ultimate destruction was made certain.

Because of Calvary Scripture can say, 'If we confess our sins, he is faithful and just and will forgive us our sins and purify us from all unrighteousness.' (1 John 1:9, NIV.) ' "Every sin and blasphemy will be forgiven men." ' (Matthew 12:31, NIV.) ' "If anyone is thirsty, let him come to me and drink. Whoever believes in me, as the Scripture has said, streams of living water will flow from within him." ' (John 7:37, 38, NIV.) ' "Whoever is thirsty, let him come; and whoever wishes, let him take the free gift of the water of life." ' (Revelation 22:17, NIV.)

Jesus made the unconditional promise: 'Him that cometh to me I will in no wise cast out.' John 6:37. Anyone, anywhere, any time who comes to Jesus is always, always, always accepted.

But could that promise possibly include the 'queen of the black witches', someone who had 'sold her soul to Satan'?

CHAPTER TWELVE

HELL'S FOUNDATIONS QUIVER

A warm long-shadowed summer evening on a Bristol street corner. Daring Diana, high on drink and drugs, dressed to kill, was waiting for a client. Crowds of Bible-carriers surged towards Colston Hall. 'All the religious hypocrites going to Eric Hutchings's meeting,' she thought.

Without warning her temper again touched ten on the Richter scale. Rational thought banished, she followed the crowd with one objective: to get to the front of that meeting and use her long nails on Hutchings's face so that even his mother wouldn't recognize him.

She does not recall how it happened but, inside Colston Hall, somebody managed to calm her down and even *sit* her down at the end of a packed row. Some stared at her; it was *that* obvious that she was a prostitute. She stared right back.

The service began. She experienced the severest discomfort. Rendered tough by a hard-scrabble life, feelings like embarrassment were foreign to her. What she was feeling now was fathoms deeper than embarrassment. A soloist began to sing.

> I would love to tell you what I think of Jesus,
> Since I found in Him a friend so strong and true,
> I would tell you how He changed my life completely,
> He's done something that no other friend could do.
>
> All my life was full of sin, when Jesus found me.
> All my life was full of misery and woe.
> Jesus placed His strong and loving arms around me,
> And He led me in the way I ought to go.

No one ever cared for me like Jesus.
There's no other Friend so kind as He.
No one else could take the sin and darkness from me.
Oh! how much He cares for me!

Doreen's whole life passed before her as it is said to do
when someone faces death.

Deep forces strove inside her. She was a common prostitute, a drug addict and a witch. She had participated in
wickedness and obscenities beyond words to describe. How
could *He* care for her? She had even made a pact and sold
her soul to Satan. How could God's love extend to her?

Yet, over the sordid, horrendous, scenes of her life —
Someone with nail-pierced hands was reaching out, now,
here.

There was the drug haze, but the familiar voices of the
spirits were not getting through in here. Another Voice was
speaking to her consciousness. A message was breaking
though:

*His hands pierced for the wrong things her hands had
done.*

His feet spiked for the wandering paths her feet had trod.

*His brow thorn-crushed for the wrong thoughts her mind
had harboured.*

*His heart broken for the wrong things her heart had
loved.*

*His side spear-riven to prove that the way to God was
wide open — even for her.*

*God 'made him to be sin for us, who knew no sin; that
we might be made the righteousness of God in him.*
2 Corinthians 5:21.

Jesus, the tender Saviour who died in her place was
driving a phrase through her befuddled mind: 'No one else
could take the sin and darkness from me.'

'If you do not know the Lord Jesus as your personal
Saviour you are BOUND . . . ,' the preacher was saying.

To everyone's consternation Doreen leapt to her feet and
shrieked, 'He's right. I AM bound!'

Stunned silence from the congregation, but Hutchings carried on.

There was an appeal at the end of the sermon: 'Come to Jesus tonight. . . .' The choir began singing:

> Just as I am — without one plea,
> But that thy blood was shed for me,
> And that thou bid'st me come to thee,
> O Lamb of God, I come, I come!

It was then that Doreen heard the audible voice of Diablos: 'You are MINE. You cannot go. It's too late for you. You are MINE.'

The devil had a most fearful struggle on his hands. The choir was still singing:

> Just as I am — though tossed about
> With many a conflict, many a doubt
> Fightings and fears within, without —
> O Lamb of God, I come, I come!

Diablos was losing his slave. Doreen was reaching for the nail-scarred hands.

'I'm coming, Jesus,' she said quietly. 'Please take the darkness away.'

Anywhere else Satan might have physically prevented her from moving. Used terror to stop her getting to the front of that hall. But present here was a Power far greater than his — and he knew it!

Nevertheless, right there at the front she heard the voice of Satan say, 'You cannot change. You are MINE.'

Certainly there were practical problems to be faced. Her way of life. Her drug problem.

At the front of the hall she dare not tell the counsellors *all* about her past. She just said, 'I'm a drug addict.' How was she to know that they would not dream of turning her away no matter what she had been?

Mrs. Mary Hutchings took her in hand. 'I will pray for you, my dear,' she said.

She was gentle and kind. Doreen had not met her sort before.

Well after midnight, clutching a copy of John's gospel, she left the hall.

A gaggle of prostitutes was standing at the corner near Colston Hall. They must have sensed what had happened, and couldn't believe it.

Doreen showed them her copy of John's gospel and bade them good night.

Tears coursed down her painted face.

She had taken her first step to freedom.

The following morning the problems poured over her. How could she possibly live a Christian life? Give up drugs, drink and the way of life on the streets? She heard the audible voice of the devil saying: 'You can't get out of it; you're mine! It's too late for *you*.'

It is, she thought. And made for the nearest pub. But even as she drank she heard the voice of the soloist:

No one else could take the sin and darkness from me.
Oh! how much He cares for me!

She went on the streets in search of men but the words of the song kept replaying in her memory.

Again the audible voice of Satan, 'It's not for you.'

But there were two voices speaking to her now. They were saying opposite things. It appeared she had a choice. On the one hand, the powers of darkness. On the other hand, Jesus Christ, the mighty Son of God.

'Keep away from Christians, or you will die,' growled Satan.

A woman counsellor visited her in her flat. She explained the 'how to' of the new birth. Gave her the address of an evangelical church.

Doreen will never forget her first experience of attending a church. For one thing she couldn't understand a word the preacher was saying. He spoke in such long words and theological phrases. Nothing was simple or plain. She wanted to hear something about Jesus that she could understand.

For all that, she had an opportunity to pray.

Afterwards at the church door she told the preacher that she had given her heart to Jesus at Colston Hall. He beamed. She decided to shock him. She told him she was a prostitute and a drug addict. But he only smiled, asked her to come again, and asked her how he and his team could help her.

Long weeks of struggle were ahead for Doreen. At one moment she would be tearing a Bible to shreds. At another she would remember everything and repeat the words, 'Knock, and it *shall* be opened unto you.' At another moment she would be screaming, hissing and slithering along the floor like a snake. On frequent occasions she ran out of church screaming.

Through all this Jesus kept speaking to her. The Holy Spirit was breaking through.

Meanwhile the devil was using every means at his disposal to drive her to suicide.

At a Baptist meeting she overpowered two ministers who were trying to pray and lay hands on her. They contacted the Revd Arthur Neil. In a harrowing series of encounters in his home, Neil, in the name of Jesus Christ and in the power of His Holy Spirit, cast the demons out of her. The tormentors left her with loud screams.

'Jesus is Victor!' exclaimed Neil. 'Jesus is Victor!'

The evil spirits had gone for ever. Temptations continued. But victory had been won at a cross on a green hill. And through the power of this cross and of the resurrection Doreen now had the power of choice. Her choice: to walk the risen life with Jesus.

After a period in a retreat centre in Bedfordshire, Doreen returned to start a new life in Bristol. She began an active programme of witnessing. But the people who had known her before didn't recognize her now. She was so changed. She dressed differently, spoke differently and acted differently. She *was* different: a new creature in Christ.

When the word got around among the prostitutes they would shout out, 'Look out! Here comes Diana with her Jesus leaflets!' But Doreen would reply, 'Diana is dead. You will never see her again.'

At church she heard the minister read Paul's epistle to the Romans chapter 8 verses 38 and 39:

'For I am persuaded, that neither death, nor life, nor angels, nor principalities, nor powers, nor things present, nor things to come, nor height, nor depth, nor any other creature, shall be able to separate us from the love of God, which is in Christ Jesus our Lord.'

'*Nor witch, nor Satanist,*' Doreen added.

Doreen is happily married now and has a family. Hundreds of times she has had the joy of giving her testimony at Christian meetings. Her book, *From Witchcraft to Christ* (Concordia), has gone through many printings.

'In the past ten years', says Doreen, 'witchcraft, Satanism, Spiritualism, and other evil cults have trebled in number. The occult has spread over the world like a malignant cancer. I feel it my duty to warn against such grossly evil practices, for I have met young people whose lives have been ruined by getting mixed up with dark and evil things.'

Doreen has kept her East End accent. Except for deep, intense eyes which have their own story, she looks ordinary enough.

But there is nothing ordinary about Doreen Irvine. At *her* conversion Hell's foundations quivered.

CHAPTER THIRTEEN

DENOUEMENT

The story of the 'queen of the black witches' has a 'happy ending'.

Do *all* stories of occult involvement have happy endings?

Sadly, no. A huge proportion of those who become involved in the occult — witchcraft, Satanism, spiritualism — end their lives in suicide or in insane asylums.

What of the case studies we have examined? Kate the medium terrorized by the spectres of hell? Will Baron, New Age channeller, committed to infiltrating Christian congregations? Johanna Michaelsen of 'Mind Control' and Pachita, the spirit-possessed healer? None of these stories is finished yet. We can only tell them up to the present. At present not all end in victory and new birth.

'For our struggle is not against flesh and blood, but against the rulers, against the authorities, against the powers of this dark world and against the spiritual forces of evil. . . . Therefore put on the full armour of God, so that when the day of evil comes, you may be able to stand your ground, and after you have done everything, to stand.' Ephesians 6:12, 13, NIV.

With those whose lives are committed to Jesus, even with those who have not in some way invited His interference in their lives, Satan is *not* at liberty to use the terrors of his dark world.

But there is always temptation.

No one is exempt from temptation.

The second-born person *will* be tempted.

What Paul calls 'the old man of sin' is not taken away at conversion. It is neutralized as we look to Jesus and for as long as we look to Jesus. If we take our eyes from Jesus it will seek to take over. We are 'in Jesus', 'in the Spirit', but the 'flesh' is 'in' us and, with divine help, we must fight it all the day long. If our failures are but slips on the road to glory there is pardon (1 John 1:9) and 'no condemnation' because we are 'in Christ Jesus' (Romans 8:1).

But what if, once again, through the freedom of choice which is our birthright, we should again *choose* to make sin a way of life . . . ? (See Hebrews 10:26, 27.)

After her devil-driven suicidal depressions, Kate left her lover and returned to Keith. She began a conscious search for Jesus Christ as the only alternative to the chamber of psychic horrors that had been her life.

Her search for Jesus seemed to lead nowhere — until Kate became involved with a Bible study group. An appointment was made for her to meet a Christian minister.

On the night before, with Keith away on a business trip, Satan made a determined attempt to hold on to Kate.

It was to be the longest night of her life.

Now there were no tactics of terror. The being in Kate's bedroom was the tall, sensuous magnetic figure she had seen on two previous occasions. Kate believes that it was Satan himself. She felt that had she fixed her gaze upon him her battle against devilry, darkness and depression would have been lost, together with the light and hope she was beginning to find in Jesus. But certain things make devils tremble. And, in her battle that night, Kate had a mighty Helper.

Kate survived to meet the Christian pastor.

For the first time she told her full story. He listened in silence. Then he pointed Kate to the good news about Jesus Christ set out in the gospels and by the apostle Paul in the book of Romans.

Kate discovered that all have sinned and come short of the glory of God. She found that the sacrifice of Christ on Calvary's cross was enough to wash away every confessed sin, even hers. She discovered that the power of Christ brings transformation, peace, joy, life to the full and freedom from fear of the powers of darkness which had held her in thrall for so long.

Kate found that through the good news about Jesus Christ — His sinless life, His blameless death, His glorious resurrection — can come freedom, victory and eternal life to all who believe.

Kate does not smile easily. And she did not smile then.

'I sense you are happy,' said the pastor.

Kate was more than happy; she had found the peace and the joy that passes all understanding.

That night she poured out her soul to the Saviour. Her sins were confessed and washed away. Transformation began. Kate's prayer concluded with these words: 'Lord Jesus; Keith and I have come through so much. Don't let it be you who comes between us now.'

Kate invited Keith to accompany her to her new church. To her surprise, he complied, muttering to himself, 'Here we go again. . . .'

But matter-of-fact, feet-on-the-ground Keith was in for a shock. At Kate's church he heard the good news about Jesus Christ presented in a way he had never heard it before. He decided that he wanted the same peace and joy Kate had found.

Kate and Keith were baptized.

For two years things went well. On my visits to their home I sensed the presence of Jesus. Little Carol was now quite a young lady, full of life, showing no signs of the problems that had afflicted her earlier. The home where evil angels once dwelt was at peace now. No bloodless hands rapped upon doors. No footsteps on the stairs in the hours of darkness. There were no apparitions. Peace and the presence of God reigned supreme.

Kate no longer wanted to die. From the valley of the shadow of death she had been recalled to life.

Kate confesses she sometimes falls down. 'The sin problem is not taken away when you are born again,' she says. 'The devil does not give up trying.'

But Kate had been justified, forgiven, released. Daily, through prayer, the guilt of sin was removed from her life. She was growing to maturity in Jesus.

'I am looking towards Jesus,' she told me. 'He increases in my life, and self decreases; the power of sin is waning. But the *presence* of sin is still there like a traitor lurking in the shadows. I suppose it will be like that as long as I have this passion-ridden body. Until Jesus returns in glory. . . .'

I should like to end the story of Kate right here. But I feel I must tell you the rest.

Satan began a subtle attack on the congregation of which Kate and Keith had become members. He introduced a fifth column.

An Australian doctor based at a private sanatorium came to preach locally. He brought with him a book he had written and cassette tapes that he and others had made. His doctrine was perfectionism: the belief that the Christian must achieve absolute character perfection in order to be saved. He spoke much about the law and standards of conduct. Like the New Agers he took Christian terms and made them mean something different.

In the privacy of their own home Kate and Keith read his book, the most subtle mix of truth and error Satan could devise. They felt that character perfection was a higher plane to which God was calling them.

With tears the pastor pleaded, 'There is room for everyone at the foot of the cross. There is room for only Jesus *on* the cross. You cannot deserve, achieve your own salvation, make your own atonement. "For by grace are ye saved through faith; and that not of yourselves: it is the gift of God: not of works, lest any man should boast." Ephesians 2:8, 9.'

Kate and Keith went back to the Australian guru and he dismissed the pastor's arguments with the words, 'Cheap grace'. They returned to the pastor; 'Cheap grace? No. The grace of Christ is not cheap, *it is free*. Our only chance of salvation is through the blood (the righteousness) of Christ.

That is the only way. That is the meaning of Calvary. That is why Jesus came. That is our only hope of heaven.'

Satan was working hard on the little congregation. Among those who absorbed the bleak creed of perfectionism was the lay elder and his wife. Very soon they, with Kate and Keith, were adopting a critical, judgemental attitude towards their fellow believers. Keith realized something was wrong; and so did Kate — when she, her husband and daughter Carol became the victims of the sharp, loveless, judgemental creed of the lay elder.

They stopped attending church.

The pastor pleaded. *I* pleaded. Other Christian friends pleaded. But it was to no avail; Kate and Keith had decided to strive for perfection in the isolation of their own home.

Sins over which Christ had given them the victory at conversion returned to plague them. Depression hung over Kate. After some months trying to be perfect Kate and Keith gave up the struggle — and with it their claim to be Christians. Temptations overwhelmed.

I keep in touch. The rash that covered the body of little Carol when Satan occupied the home disappeared after Kate and Keith had been baptized. It has now returned. But to the best of my knowledge God has not permitted satanic terrors to re-enter the home. Nor, according to Kate, will she ever in any way invite them to do so.

But, like the father in the story of the prodigal son, God spends His days waiting and watching the road that comes from the Far Country, hoping to see in some distant dust cloud the shapes of His returning prodigals. Ready, at a moment's notice, to rush out and embrace them, just as they are, place the kiss of justification on their cheeks, and order the garments (which represent the perfection of His Son) to be placed around their shoulders.

Will Baron was nothing if not sincere.

A New Age infiltrator into Christian congregations, still channelling for a spirit he called 'Jesus', he managed to convince himself that he was a 'Spirit-filled, born-again

Christian'. The spirit directions he was accustomed to hearing — 'Do this,' 'Go here' — he now thought came from the Holy Spirit. He believed he had 'the gift of tongues'. Looking back, Will says, 'But all this time I was still a disciple of Satan.'

Will introduced Christian congregations to his meditation techniques and, from there, sought to lead them into the occult world of New Age.

But, in using Will to infiltrate Christian congregations, Satan was taking a calculated risk. Influence can work both ways.

Back in Manchester, Will had praying parents. After being ordered by the spirits to attend a special evangelistic rally, he found someone else to pray for him. The evangelist had preached straight Gospel. There was not a hint of New Age about the whole crusade. Will was so angry at the close of the meeting that when a woman in her mid-thirties who had been sitting by the side of him asked him what kind of Christian he was, he dropped his guard. The spirits had always been insistent that he should never tell anyone of his New Age affiliation. On this occasion he blurted out, 'I am a New Age Christian.'

Quietly the woman replied, 'Yes, I understand. I used to be involved with New Age myself. That was before I found the Lord. Would you mind if I prayed for you?'

Nonplussed, Will was silent. She prayed for him aloud, there and then. When she left she announced her intention of praying for him regularly thereafter.

The substance of her prayer had been, 'Give this brother wisdom to see what is true. Let him fully understand your Word. May the mighty power of your Spirit work in his life and lead him to a knowledge of the real Jesus. Amen.'

After that it was a case of Will picking up the right books. More often than not they were right alongside New Age books in the Christian bookshops.

Will discovered the power of the New Testament. He found Revelation gripping. He read of an end-time power — antichrist — that would seek to deceive and destroy

God's true followers and masquerade as Christ. He would perform 'great and miraculous signs' and 'because of the signs' would deceive 'the inhabitants of the earth'. Revelation 13:13, 14. Clearly, in end-time, Satan would be permitted to duplicate/counterfeit powers once the special prerogative of the Holy Spirit.

He was in agonies when he realized that both Djwhal Khul and even the spirit which had identified itself as 'Jesus Christ' had been Satan's evil angels. For years he had been under the influence of demons. Demons who were part of a world-wide movement to counterfeit Christianity and use him as part of a great, international hoax. 'I suddenly understood that Satan is ultimately preparing the world for his spectacular appearance', writes Will, 'in which millions and millions of people will proclaim him to be Christ, the returned Messiah. In reality it will be the appearing of the antichrist.'

Satan and his demons had been training him as a false prophet. The 'masters of the hierarchy' had been demons masquerading as agents of God. He read Revelation 12 and, in verses 7-9, found the record of a civil war which had taken place in heaven before the creation of the world; and in verse 4 he found the implication that one third of the angelic host had rebelled with Lucifer (Satan) and had been expelled from heaven. These fallen angels had become demons; and these demons had been his constant companions for some twelve years and he, their slave.

Will Baron experienced the new birth. He went around the Christian congregations he had been used to infiltrate. He told them what he had sought to do and not one of them had been aware that they had been targets for infiltration.

For months he needed specialized counselling from Christian pastors and teachers. For several weeks he lived through the trauma of Satan's harassment and intimidation. But Satan could not succeed. He was beaten.

This is how Will concludes his story:

'I thank God I am saved through the love and grace of

Jesus Christ. I am thankful for His Word, the Bible, and for the power of prayer that reveals truth and protects us from deception and evil. . . . I rejoice that I have personally experienced the fulfilment of Jesus' promise that "the truth will set you free". (John 8:32.)' *Deceived by the New age* (Pacific Press), page 192.

From her first encounter with the occult Johanna Michaelsen's every experience ended with her acknowledging that what she had first accepted as a benign power was, in fact, an evil, threatening power. Her exposure to Hermanito was no exception. As time went on, when operations were in progress, she sensed 'the swirling presence of the spirits', and it frightened her. On several occasions she voiced objections to the singing of hymns to Hermanito and became aware that when the name of God was invoked Hermanito would mutter to himself (in Spanish), 'It is I, it is I.'

Johanna began to wonder; 'Does the fact that "miracles" *do* occur *necessarily* mean that God is involved? Given certain circumstances is it not possible for other supernatural agencies to perform miracles? Disease came into the world at the same time as evil; Satan was the source of both. He could, beyond question, cause disease. Could he also, on occasion, remove it?

Johanna needed space — and time to think. She escaped to Europe. In Switzerland she encountered Francis and Edith Schaeffer at their Christian retreat centre, *L'Abri*. For the first time in years she felt able to stand back and look at things clearly. She reviewed the development of her mongrel philosophy. She had, she said, taken whatever element happened to appeal to her from Hinduism, Spiritualism and Christianity — and casually discarded the rest.

She confided in Edith Schaeffer. Edith contrasted Hermanito's healing methods with those of Jesus. A mere word from the mouth of Jesus had been sufficient to bring about a healing miracle.

Johanna was moving in the direction of Christianity.

On the night of 15 November 1972 the power that was Hermanito finally revealed itself.

Johanna was walking alone along a slippery path near the Schaeffers' mountain retreat. She had been planning to take the train out of Switzerland but, only that morning, had changed her mind. And that change of mind had powerful implications.

Picking her way along the path she became aware that a dense, black fog had formed around her, blotting everything from view. 'The dark mist was swirling, alive, filled with the presence of something more monstrous than anything I had ever before encountered. Voices began whispering, hissing incoherent words, and there was laughter in my right ear. An ice-cold breath touched the back of my neck under my hair.

' ''Hermanito, help me,'' I gasped. The voices shrieked in hideous laughter.

' ''We're going to kill you!'' '

Something that felt like a giant fist slammed against Johanna's back between her shoulders. She pitched forward in the darkness and called out, 'Jesus, help me!'

'He can't help you,' the voices around her shrieked. 'He can't help you!'

But the blackness lifted. At the end of the path she could see the Christian centre. Soon there, she was ushered in by one of Dr. Schaeffer's colleagues.

'Can't you see them?' Johanna gasped. 'Can't you see their faces?'

'No,' said the Christian, 'but I know One who can. Satan, in the name of Jesus Christ of Nazareth, I command you to be gone! I forbid your presence here. I claim the protection of the blood of Jesus upon us. Go where Jesus sends you!'

God had permitted Johanna to see the source behind the psychic phenomena that had dogged her experience since puberty and, more recently, had in her presence performed apparent miracles. Murderous demonic rage had been the spirits' reaction to her potential decision to reach out to the *real* Jesus Christ.

Now the unseen world of the spirits was banished from her experience.

On Friday 17 November 1972 she formally renounced her involvement in the occult and committed her life to Jesus Christ as her Lord and Saviour. She would never again face the darkness alone.

CHAPTER FOURTEEN

WHEN THE WALLS FELL DOWN

But Johanna was by no means free of the darkness when she arrived back in Mexico.

For one thing her parents put considerable pressure on her to return to Mind Control and Pachita.

Johanna decided she had a lot of reading to do. Surely, she reasoned, if the Bible was a complete guide to life and its problems, it must have something to say about the psychic and how it figured in God's scheme of things.

She had not been looking long before she hit on Deuteronomy 18:9-14 (NIV). God was condemning 'detestable ways' and 'detestable practices'. These were to be avoided like the plague. 'Let no one be found among you . . . who practises divination or sorcery, interprets omens, engages in witchcraft, or casts spells, or who is a medium or spiritist or who consults the dead. Anyone who does these things is detestable to the Lord.'

It would, she thought, have been difficult for God to have made Himself any clearer. Then Johanna ran across Leviticus 20. In this passage God Himself was speaking. ' " 'I will set my face against the person who turns to mediums and spiritists to prostitute himself by following them, and I will cut him off from his people.' " ' (Verse 6.) She found that the same strictures against mediums and spiritists were repeated in even stronger terms in verse 27.

When Johanna ran across 1 John 4:1 her mind began to race. 'Dear friends, do not believe every spirit, but test the spirits to see whether they are from God. . . .' (NIV.) In no time she was setting off for Mind Control to summon her 'counsellors' and 'test the spirits'. Before long she was confronted by 'Jesus'.

Immediately she went on the offensive. 'You are not the "Jesus" of the Bible, are you?' she demanded.

No reply. His eyes were closed.

'I command you, in the name of Jesus Christ of Nazareth, tell me, Do you believe that Jesus Christ is God, uniquely incarnate in human flesh?'

A bomb seemed to explode in her Mind Control laboratory. Everything shook, most of the contents of the room were destroyed — and even the walls fell down!

When the dust had settled, her counsellors had vanished. She no longer had any questions. 'The works of the medium were abominations before God. Neither the psychic perceptions of Mind Control nor Pachita's work had its source in God,' writes Johanna in her book, *The Beautiful Side of Evil.*

Johanna prayed earnestly that her psychic susceptibilities would be removed. She made a bonfire on which she heaped all her books on the occult as well as the artefacts associated with it. A Christian pastor had explained that these had been 'focal points for the demons' who had been in her home.

In June 1973 she was involved in Campus Crusade for Christ. She met internationally-known evangelical Dr. Walter Martin. Martin taught her how to study the Bible and, at his suggestion, she began to sift through 'the depressing stack of diaries, notes and calendars' and, with his help, produced the transcript of her book. She then enrolled for an advanced course at a Bible college. It was here that, on 19 April 1976, she met Randolf. Six months later they were married in a beautiful candle-lit wedding.

Throughout her period at Bible college Johanna had continued to experience spiritual depressions. Only after her marriage, through sharing daily prayer and Bible study with her husband, did the depressions disappear. 'It takes time', she writes, 'to be transformed through the renewing of the mind.'

In the years since their marriage Johanna and Randolf Michaelsen have continued to study the Word together. With growing concern they have watched the development of the New Age movement and other occult phenomena in Western countries. They see it as an end-time sign immediately to precede the glorious return of Jesus Christ. False Christs, false prophets, contrary winds of doctrine sweeping through the church, and the spirits of devils working miracles were all to be part of the scene in the fag-end world before Jesus appeared in the vaulted heavens so that every eye could see Him. Had He not outlined the details Himself in His Olivet sermon (Matthew 24; Mark 13; Luke 21)?

'The world is being carefully groomed', writes Johanna, 'for the arrival of the one whom Scripture calls "the man of lawlessness . . . the son of destruction" (2 Thessalonians 2:3). I believe this man is in the world today and Satan is working overtime to prepare mankind to hail the satanic signs and miracles he will perform (Revelation 13:13) as being wonders from the hand of God Himself.'

Johanna believes that clergy influenced by liberal theology are doing much to prepare the ground for the New Age hoax in which Satan will seek to impersonate Christ. She cites the continued popularity of Bishop James Pike's book *The Other Side* (Doubleday) in which he recounts the seance in which he allegedly spoke to his suicide son. The bishop had asked the 'spirit of Jim', 'Have you heard anything over there about Jesus?' The spirit had answered, 'They talk about Him — a mystic, a seer, yes, a seer. Oh, but, Dad, they don't talk about Him as a Saviour. As an example, you see? . . . Not a Saviour, that's the important thing — just an example.'

With Dr. Walter Martin, Johanna Michaelsen has addressed many congregations on the subject of the occult and the New Age. She emphasizes strongly the unreliability of feelings. Her feelings had assured her that Pachita's work had been holy because the name of Jesus had been invoked and there was a crucifix on the altar. The question that must be asked, she insists, is not *Did a genuine miracle occur?* but *What is the source behind it?*

Up to his death in the summer of 1989 Johanna campaigned with Dr. Martin against the occult and the New Age.

Martin was deeply concerned that 42 per cent of Americans claim to have had contact with the dead, that a third of the US population believe in reincarnation and that fifty million Americans allow astrology to dictate their decision-making. Martin cited *Fortune* magazine as saying that half of America's 500 top businesses are engaged in New Age 'human potential training' (accepted by Christians as the entering wedge to the occult). Among the companies exposing their managements to 'New Age gurus', said Martin, were Pacific Bell (who had spent 173 million dollars on 'human potential training' for their management that involved obvious aspects of the occult), NASA, both the Ford and the General Motors car manufacturing companies, ICA, IBM, Boeing, Singer, RCA and the Bank of America. Potentially, Martin believed, this gave occult forces a stranglehold on the American economy.

He believed that the New Age was also gaining a similar control over the American media. The movies *Ghostbusters I* and *II, ET, Indiana Jones and The Temple of Doom, 2001 and Star Wars*, he asserted, were all inspired by the New Age. He believed that practically every major US publisher had gone into New Age literature contemptuous of its content but convinced that it would make money.

In one of his last TV broadcasts Dr. Martin looked at the influence of New Age on the home. '*Dungeons and dragons*' had, he said, led hundreds of children into acts of violence — and even to suicide; that many children's nursery stories were being dressed up in New Age garb.

He drew a parallel between the contemporary United States and the record of King Saul in 1 Samuel 28-31. Saul had started well but, gradually, had separated himself from God and from all godly influences — including Samuel, David, the priesthood, as well as his own better self. Finally, on the night before his fall Saul was so far from God that he had become involved with the occult: he consulted a channeller.

Saul's great protagonist had been David. Like Saul, David had been a grievous sinner. But there had been a great

difference between the two men: David had hated his sins
and repented of them. When, in 1 Kings 14:8, God had
referred to ' " 'my servant David, who kept my commands
and followed me with all his heart, doing only what was
right . . . ' " ' he had not lost his memory. David had
repented and the blood of Christ had covered his sins which,
as a consequence, had been washed away. The same course
of action had been open to Saul. He had not taken it. He
had gone the way of the occult. And, in doing so, had
abandoned hope of salvation and everlasting life.

Johanna had had something of Saul *and* something of
David in her experience. After more than twenty years surrounded by the horrors of the psychic as well as the diabolic
healing of Pachita, Johanna has encountered the *real* Jesus.
With Him she has found pardon, peace, joy and the assurance of salvation.

But something has been preoccupying her of late. Partly
it is the feeling that ideas current in popular Christian theology have made phenomena like mediumship and channelling possible. Partly it is that, through her Bible reading, and
influenced by the writings of Martin and Tony Campolo, together with Britain's John Stott and Richard Bewes, she has
come seriously to question the still popular going-to-heaven-
or-going-to-hell view of the nature of man in death.

When we met at the Frankfurt Book Fair, Johanna told me
that she believed that the key to a proper understanding of
the biblical view of the nature of man in death was found
in the story of the raising of Lazarus. . . .

CHAPTER FIFTEEN

THE FINAL CURTAIN?

Lazarus, it will be recalled, died. His story is in John 11. He didn't just lapse into a coma, and he wasn't on some life support machine. He was as dead as a man could be. So dead, in fact, that they buried him. They put him in a cave and rolled a great stone in front of it, after carefully preparing his body and wrapping it in the grave-clothes customary at the time.

So it can be well and truly said that Lazarus was dead. But Jesus, his friend, came to the cemetery in Bethany and said, 'Lazarus, come out.' Lazarus 'came out'. Always the practical man, Jesus then gave orders that he should be freed from the impedimenta of the grave and restored to his sisters. There was great rejoicing. Needless to say, Jesus was a welcome guest at the Lazarus house and had a special place in the hearts of the family ever after.

And here we encounter the problem. Christians can accept the death of Lazarus and, by faith, his resurrection. But over the centuries there is one thing they have found it very diffi-cult to understand: *the silence of Lazarus.*

According to popular theology the soul of Lazarus should, at the point of death, have been freed from his body and found lodgement in heaven or hell. Having been a man of faith, it has tended to be assumed that the soul of Lazarus would have found lodgement in heaven. For four days he was a corpse. Before his resurrection his sisters made it clear to Jesus that decay and decomposition had already set in. His soul, therefore, should have quite positively left for realms afar.

But Jesus came and called him back. Back from where? From the boulevards of paradise where he had been wander-ing with awe for four days? Had that been the case would not Lazarus have betrayed just a little impatience at being snatched back to this vale of tears when he had had the sublime taste of the delights of heavenly ecstasy? Why didn't he say, 'Oh Master, why didn't you leave me where I was? Why did you recall me to this place where I must always endure pain and sorrow and hardship — even though it is good to see my sisters again?'

And that is not the only mysterious thing for Christians about the silence of Lazarus. Why didn't he now begin to tell of all the marvellous things he had seen and experienced? To tell everyone, 'Don't get upset at the prospect of death; heaven makes it worth while'?

No such ecstasy broke from the lips of the resurrected Lazarus; neither were there any such recriminations for being deprived of the bliss that only heaven can offer. Why the silence? A conspiracy of silence, perhaps? Was Jesus party to his silence about what Lazarus saw when he was light years away in heaven? Would Christ have brought Lazarus back to tread the dusty roads of this sin-cursed cosmos if Lazarus had, in fact, been enjoying the marvels of heaven?

Is it possible that the reason for the silence of Lazarus is that Lazarus saw nothing in heaven? That he wasn't travelling the golden streets or sitting at the feet of angels?

Before he went to raise Lazarus, Jesus told His disciples that Lazarus was sleeping (John 11:11-14). Is that significant? Is that what death is? A dreamless sleep, nothing more, nothing less? The sister of Lazarus didn't expect to see her brother until the resurrection day when all the righteous will be raised (verse 24). She said so. She didn't think for one moment that Lazarus was in paradise. She didn't imagine that some intangible 'soul' was wafting its triumphant flight through the realms of glory. If she had imagined this, would she have pleaded that Lazarus be brought back to life?

Was Lazarus silent about what happened in those four days for the simple reason that nothing happened to him in those four days? That his body simply began the process of returning to the dust from which mankind is created?

That when he was restored to life that process was halted and reversed as Christ restored to him the breath of life? Well, it's a point of view . . . .

When evangelical thought-leader John Stott came out against Hell the sparks began to fly!

Quite soon Dr. Stott was on the defensive; he wanted 'to repudiate with all the vehemence of which I am capable, the glibness, which almost appears to be the glee' with which some evangelicals held on to hell. *Essentials* (Hodder and Stoughton), page 312.

Where Hell came from. In the seminaries, colleges and universities, Stott's views shocked no one. The scholars were prepared. Professor John Hick, for example, had researched the whole business of what happens after death. He published his findings — first in 1976; revised edition 1985 — in a mammoth tome titled *Death and Eternal Life* (MacMillan). Uncomfortable as we may find some of his evidence, intellectual honesty compels us to weigh it.

The evidence of archaeology, said Hick, was that Hell and survival after death as a 'shade . . . in a dim underworld' were ideas thousands of years old. Along with reincarnation and the belief that man has an 'immortal soul' these ideas belonged to primal religion. Stonehenge and all that.

From Homer's *Iliad, Odyssey* and elsewhere, Hick demonstrates that these primal beliefs were absorbed into the culture of ancient Greece. The Greeks, he said, believed that the 'soul' was 'the body's shadow image'; at death it went down into Hades (Hell) where it persisted as a 'depleted, joyless entity, a mere bloodless shadow of its former self' (page 58).

The Greeks then, Hick demonstrated, taught these ideas to the Romans. And, on the eve of Emperor Constantine's conversion to Christianity, these views were held throughout the Empire.

In contrast to the Primal-Greek-Roman view, discovered Hick, was the view of life after death present in Hebrew and, later, early Christian literature: the Old and New Testaments.

By the time of Daniel the idea of Resurrection was firmly fixed. With the single exception of the Sadducee party, this was the view accepted by Jews at the time of Jesus. With the Resurrection view, says Hick, there were variations; 'Sometimes the righteous are to be resurrected to a kingdom established on this present earth; sometimes it is on a "purified" or renewed earth.' (Pages 71 and 172.)

Hick demonstrates that Jesus reinforced the Resurrection view both in argument — and by being resurrected! The resurrection of Jesus, he says, was not the *sole ground* of early Christian belief in resurrection. They believed the Old Testament and the statements of Jesus. Nevertheless it was a guarantee that they themselves would be resurrected at the Last Day, at the end of all things. This Last Day was equated with the return of Jesus.

The Second Coming. The idea of the second coming of Jesus is present, on average, once in every twenty-five New Testament verses. It is a belief which has enjoyed a revival among Christians since World War II. The report of The International Evangelical Leaders' Consultation which met at Grand Rapids, USA, in 1982 contained this sentence: 'We all agreed that our Christian hope focuses on the personal, visible and glorious return of our Lord Jesus Christ, on the resurrection from the dead, and on the perfected kingdom which His appearance will bring.' (Cited *Essentials*, page 275.)

Even before this affirmation of belief in the second advent, evangelical Anglicans like John Stott, David Watson and Richard Bewes had been preaching the glorious return. In doing so, inescapably, they had been using those passages of New Testament Scripture which also deal with the resurrection of the dead. Among them was Paul's first letter to the Thessalonians (written in AD 51) chapter 4, verses 13-17.

'Brothers, we do not want you to be ignorant about those who fall asleep, or to grieve like the rest of men, who have no hope. We believe that Jesus died and rose again and so we believe that God will bring with Jesus those who have fallen asleep in him. According to the Lord's own word, we tell you that we who are still alive, who are left till the coming of the Lord, will certainly not precede those who have fallen asleep. For the Lord himself will come down from heaven, with a loud command, with the voice of the archangel and with the trumpet call of God, and the dead in Christ will rise first. After that, we who are still alive and are left will be caught up with them in the clouds to meet the Lord in the air. And so we will be with the Lord for ever.' (NIV.)

In their second advent preaching, the evangelicals have been careful to follow the details of this scenario set out by Paul. In addition they have used Christ's Olivet sermon to emphasize Jesus' 'belief that his coming would be a global, divine and cataclysmic climax to history' not a localized happening (*Essentials*, page 309). The emphasis of Jesus and of the apostles, Stott has written, was on the unexpectedness of the return and on the consequent need for watchfulness (page 312).

Where the evangelicals have come into controversy has been, first, on the Resurrection and the nature of man in death suggested in the New Testament passages; and, second, on the nature of Hell.

Death and resurrection. Back to Professor Hick and that mammoth tome.

Hick has found evidence that the Primal-Greek-Roman idea of 'the immortality of the soul' was beginning to be absorbed by the Christian church at the end of the second century, that it subsequently came to be accepted as Roman church dogma and that the majority of Protestant scholars failed to identify it as non-biblical at the time of the Reformation. *Death and Eternal Life* (MacMillan), pages 178, 179-180.

Only in recent controversies, says Hick, has 'the immortality of the soul' been challenged by mainstream Protestant scholars. The alternative view is that, in death, man 'sleeps' until he is awoken by Christ at the time of His second advent (pages 182, *et seq*).

Conscientious scholars like John Stott and Professor Hick have searched both testaments in vain for evidence of an immortal soul. In their search they have uncovered verses like Ezekiel 18:4, 'The soul that sinneth, it shall die,' and Revelation 16:3, 'Every living soul died.' As they leafed through their Old Testaments they found many references to souls being 'cut off with the sword'.

In the end, facts had to be faced. The words translated 'soul' and 'spirit' occurred 1,642 times in the Bible and, further, that that represented 1,642 opportunities for an explanation that a 'soul' or 'spirit' can function consciously without a body. But not one text said that. John Cooper wrote his book, *Body, Soul and Life Everlasting*, to support the traditional view. Nevertheless, on page 47, he says this: 'There are no texts in which soul or spirit or person must be interpreted as an immaterial substance that functions independent of the body.' For this reason many scholars have reached the conclusion that soul or spirit seem either to refer to the whole 'psycho-physical person or otherwise the energizing life-force given by God'.

In Genesis 2:7 God, having created man, is described as making him a 'living soul' by breathing breath into his body. This would tend to suggest that body plus breath equals soul.

But what did Jesus teach? In John 5:28 and 29 He said, 'The hour is coming, in the which all that are in the graves shall hear his voice, and shall come forth; they that have done good, unto the resurrection of life; and they that have done evil, unto the resurrection of damnation.'

Traditionally it has been argued that Jesus was merely speaking of the body. However, in no instance when the Bible speaks of resurrection does it distinguish between the person and the body. When they came looking for Jesus on that first Easter morning they heard the words, 'He is not here, for he is risen.' He *had* been there — until the resurrection. Later He would say to Mary, 'Touch me not for I am not yet ascended to my Father.'

In John 6:54 Jesus says, 'Whoso eateth my flesh, and

drinketh my blood, hath eternal life; and I will raise him up at the last day.' Raise him up, notice; not bring him down.

Both the Old and New Testaments call death a sleep. This happens sixty-one times. In sound sleep there is no consciousness. In Psalm 146:3 and 4 it is made very clear that, when man's breath leaves his body, 'he returneth to his earth; in that very day his thoughts perish'. 'The dead praise not the Lord, neither any that go down into silence.' Psalm 115:17. 'For the living know that they shall die: but the dead know not any thing. . . . Their love, and their hatred, and their envy, is now perished.' Ecclesiastes 9:5, 6. 'He that goeth down to the grave . . . shall return no more to his house, neither shall his place know him any more.' Job 7:9, 10.

In the passage in 1 Thessalonians 4 where Paul specifically addresses the question of death and resurrection he is concerned to reassure the anxious. What an opportunity he had, if he wanted to take it, to say, 'Don't worry. They're at home with the Lord.' Does he say that? He tells them that they do not grieve as those without hope; and that those who die, believing in Jesus, will rise again when He returns in power and great glory. In the last part of verse 16 he emphasizes, 'The dead in Christ will rise.' *Rise*, notice; not descend. The whole burden of this passage is this. What happened to Jesus, the Head of the church, happens to every member of the church. He died and God brought Him from the grave. We die and, if we have accepted His sacrifice on our behalf, God will raise us up when Jesus returns.

Oscar Cullmann in *Immortality of the Soul or Resurrection of the Dead?* (Epworth Press) expresses the two contrasting views very clearly. 'The whole of the New Testament is governed by belief in the resurrection. Belief in the immortality of the soul is not belief in a revolutionary event. Immortality, in fact, is only a *negative* assertion: the soul does *not* die, but simply lives on. Resurrection is a *positive* assertion: the whole man, who has really died, is recalled to life by a new act of creation by God. Something has happened — a miracle of creation! For something has also happened previously, something fearful: life formed by God has been destroyed.'

Hell fire and all that. John Stott has attracted a lot of flak since he came out against hell. Many of those who have attacked his views have done so without a careful examination of the evidence.

William Tyndale, the sixteenth-century's Bible translator, like Stott, could never have been accused of not examining the evidence. His conclusion was this: 'In putting your souls in purgatory, or hell, or heaven at death you have destroyed three of the central teachings of Scripture: the resurrection, the second coming, and the day of judgement.'

The resurrection is a doctrine that has brought relief to many. Those who believe in an ever-burning hell have to think the unthinkable; that many of their nearest and dearest are being burnt without relief.

The doctrine of the second coming offers hope to a hopeless world. 'Let not your heart be troubled . . . ,' said Jesus, 'I will come again, and receive you unto myself; that where I am, there ye may be also.' John 14:1, 3.

The doctrine of judgement runs right through Scripture. And the belief that, one day, all wrongs will be righted is a consolation to millions today who now suffer injustice. But the Bible doesn't say that everyone will be judged individually at death. Paul says we all must stand before the judgement seat of Christ. And we shall stand there together.

So, are there *no* scriptures to support the idea of an everburning hell?

Jude 7 says that Sodom and Gomorrah were destroyed by 'eternal fire'. If that's part of the evidence for hell it's not very convincing. The Dead Sea now covers the site of the cities of the plain. 'Eternal fire' was eternal in only one sense: *its effect*.

Malachi 4:1 speaks of evil doers being burned like chaff. How does chaff burn? Just a puff, and it's gone.

In Matthew 25:41, speaking of the irredeemably wicked, Jesus said: 'Then shall he say also unto them on his left hand, Depart from me, ye cursed, into everlasting fire.' But reference to the Greek text leads us in this, as in every other instance, in the opposite direction from the idea of an everlasting holocaust. Instead there is the idea that the *results* of the fire of judgement are permanent, everlasting.

Eternal death is not a painful form of eternal life.

Because of the ingrained concept of hell drawn from paganism God has been given a bad press by His friends down the centuries. Could it be that the whole idea of an endlessly burning hell is just an attack on the character of God — dreamed up by the arch-fiend himself? The arch-fiend who, in Eden, planted the seed that would grow into the 'immortality of the soul' belief when he said, 'Ye shall not surely die'. Genesis 3:4.

The Bible verse dealing with the destruction of the wicked is Revelation 20:9: 'And fire came down from God out of heaven, and devoured them.' But that fire, like the fire that destroyed Sodom, will go out as soon as it has done its work. It won't keep burning. God isn't like that!

John Stott makes out a conclusive case against Hell in *Essentials* (Hodder and Stoughton) pages 306-331. And Christendom owes him a debt of gratitude.

In conclusion, then. How does a belief in death as a sleep to be broken only at the resurrection when Christ returns affect the claims of the occult world?

The voice that spoke and the force that shook that room of mucho machos was not the spirit of Jeff. The spirit is merely the breath. And, in any case, Jeff was dead, totally unconscious, asleep, unaware — and will remain so until the end of all things.

For the same reason the force that haunted Bishop Pike had nothing to do with his suicide son Jim. Jim was dead, unconscious, asleep. . . .

The terrors that haunted Kate and Keith had nothing to do with the spirits of dead people.

Whatever it was that possessed Pachita that remarkable 'healer' had nothing to do with the spirit of a dead Aztec prince.

The spectres called up at Mind Control, the spirit guides that possess New Age channellers, and the voices that speak through spiritualist mediums have nothing to do with dead people.

We are back to those angels turned demons, the fallen angels, the rebel angels who were cast out of heaven. These are the deceivers of the occult world. These are the spirit impersonators. These are the lying spirits pretending to conduct an answering service on behalf of the dead.

'They are the spirits of devils, working miracles.' Revelation 16:14.

CHAPTER SIXTEEN

WHEN YOU WANT OUT

Pretty conclusive proof, yes? Enough evidence, at least, to be worthy of serious consideration.

If you toss a ball across the wall of the unseen world and it comes back with a family secret written on it, it doesn't prove that your late-lamented Uncle Laurie tossed it back. He's asleep until the resurrection. It may only prove that demons can write.

But what can be done for those who feel the mesmeric magnetism of the murky, dim-lit, diabolic domain of the occult?

Fascination with the occult. To begin with; *Why* do they feel this magnetism?

Could it be that there really is 'a God-shaped blank in everyone's mind' as G. B. Shaw said there was? That 'when men cease believing in God, they don't believe in nothing, they believe in anything' as G. K. Chesterton said they did? Is it possible that 'when God was thrown out of the window all kinds of other gods' came in as Billy Graham believes?

Man was made by God, for God. That is why he needs something greater than himself to relate to and revere. Modern materialism does not satisfy; when every last consumer durable has been installed man realizes that he has amassed no more than a heap of 'things'.

The materialism of the once Communist countries has made Eastern Europeans and others search for Christ. There are at least seventy million Christians in the USSR and fifty million in China. It was the Christians who toppled the old regimes in Eastern Europe.

In theory, then, there should be a revival of Christianity in Western lands as a reaction to the market-centred society in which Yuppie is king. And there is in some places. But elsewhere the Church is dead, thanks largely to the influence on clergy of liberal theology. It appears to have nothing to offer.

Dull lives and dull jobs cause many to reach out to the occult for thrills, only to be confronted by terrors. They should be reaching out for Christ. Unrelieved grief caused by death in the family also leads some into the occult. They would rather believe in the sanity-shaking world of shadows offered by the spirits than the God of the Hell-fire preachers. God's reputation has suffered much in the house of His friends!

To some, witchcraft and Satanism offer the power over others for which they yearn. When society is disintegrating, families coming apart in alternate houses, there is, perhaps, a sinister satisfaction in belonging to a group banded together by secret rites. But, as we have seen, God condemns the occult in terms that cannot be misunderstood. And the Bible identifies the forces behind occult phenomena as demons, the forces of evil involved in the final phase of the controversy against the forces of good and God.

Why the Bible bans the occult. Perhaps we should recap on the reasons why God takes such a strong line against all occult involvement.

1. Occult involvement means putting yourself under the control of a power that is not from God and is, in fact, in rebellion against God.

2. This God-opposing power may, in the short term, offer fascination but, in the long term, it will bring terror and — most likely — depression, insanity and suicide. The archfiend is out to destroy you.

3. Russ Parker, in *The Occult: Deliverance from Evil* (IVP) page 41, indicates that among the seven principles to which an individual has to subscribe to be admitted to the National Spiritualist Church is the necessity to become perfect in this life in order to avoid an ever-burning hell in the next. To the spiritualist Jesus was merely an Example, not a Saviour. The spiritualist must save himself from his sins, make his own atonement; 'None can shuffle out of that atonement by

an appeal to some vicarious sacrifice.' This belief is as destructive to sanity and conducive to misery, depression and ugly personalities among spiritualists as it has been among those pseudo-Christian groups who have, in practice, espoused the like theology.

4. Surrender to the occult is hateful to God because it is straight disobedience. It is not by accident that witchcraft and immorality are so often mentioned in the same breath. (Galatians 5:20; Revelation 9:21; Revelation 2:14; 1 Corinthians 10:6-9; Acts 15:29.) Power over women is one of the avowed aims of magic. Naked dances and multiple intercourse are regular features of witchcraft.

5. The longing for power to dominate and control the supernatural which lies within magic is the very opposite of the proper attitude of the creature to the Creator. 'What does the Lord require of you? To act justly and to love mercy and to walk humbly with your God.' Micah 6:8, NIV. In any event, no human ever controls the dark world of the evil supernatural. That world, quite soon, comes to control the human.

6. The desire for knowledge not normally available to man is the driving force in astrology and fortune-telling. It is an attempt to bypass the boundaries God has set. In the prophetic content of Scripture God has given to man the broad outlines of the future. And the Bible contains all that is necessary to bring about man's salvation now, so that when the culmination of history arrives he can stand with the right.

How to recognize the phoney. To those dabbling in the occult the Bible says, 'Test the spirits.' 1 John 4:1. How do we 'test the spirits' in practice?

1. 'To the law and to the testimony: if they speak not according to this word, it is because there is no light in them.' Isaiah 8:20. The first test of the prophet or healer is in the area of doctrine: What does he or she believe about Jesus Christ? Does he cling to Jesus Christ as God the Son, second person of the Trinity, God incarnate in human flesh; does he believe that Jesus was and is the God-man who

died upon the cross in our place for the forgiveness of our sins? Does he accept Him as the one born of a virgin whose physical resurrection from the dead proclaimed His victory over sin, death and Satan? Does he believe that it is 'by grace you have been saved, through faith — and this not from yourselves, it is the gift of God — not by works, so that no one can boast'? Ephesians 2:8, NIV. Or does he, through some subtle redefinition, come to accept 'another Jesus', 'another spirit', 'another gospel'?

This is how you can recognize the 'spirit of God': 'Every spirit that acknowledges that Jesus Christ has come in the flesh is from God, but every spirit that does not acknowledge Jesus is not from God. This is the spirit of the antichrist, which you have heard is coming and even now is already in the world.' 1 John 4:2, 3, NIV.

Jesus said, ' "Whoever accepts my commandments and obeys them is the one who loves me. My Father will love whoever loves me; I too will love him and reveal myself to him." ' John 14:21, GNB. It is not enough to mouth the words of our love for Jesus while practising those things which are contrary to his written Word.

2. They must be 100 per cent accurate, 100 per cent of the time. 'You may say to yourselves, "How can we know when a message has not been spoken by the Lord?" If what a prophet proclaims in the name of the Lord does not take place or come true, that is a message the Lord has not spoken. That prophet has spoken presumptuously.' Deuteronomy 18:21, 22, NIV. The 'prophets' of today, like Jean Dixon and Anne Owen, have a tendency towards inaccuracy. Even Nancy Reagan's astrologer had a great many bad days when 'the vibrations weren't just right'. The word from God is this: They must be 100 per cent on target.

3. The fact that a miracle has taken place is no guarantee whatever that God is involved. The fact that accurate information is being conveyed from 'the other side' is no guarantee that God is involved. If a miracle or sign or prophecy or healing is performed by an occultist, or by means of occult techniques, it is not from God.

4. In Deuteronomy 18:9-14 God makes His position on the occult very clear, providing a comprehensive list of the whole kit and caboodle of occult practices. He labels them all 'detestable and abominable'.

5. The Bible makes it clear that the true follower of God is conspicuous by the 'fruit' he yields, the life he lives. Romans 7:4; James 3:17, 18; Hebrews 12:11; Galatians 5:22, 23; John 15:1-8; Luke 6:43, 44, NIV. 'By their fruit you will recognize them.' Matthew 7:16, NIV. These words of Jesus are both a test and an assurance. The majority of modern false prophets and gurus are noted for their lavish, over-the-top, raunchy lives — however much whitewash they may apply to the surface for public viewing. Having said that, however, let us remember that *other* warning of Jesus (Matthew 7:15); ' "Watch out for false prophets. They come to you in sheep's clothing, but inwardly they are ferocious wolves." ' With that proviso, however, the test of verse 16 still applies.

6. We are equipped through the Word of God. But, thus equipped, we must have a day-by-day, ongoing relationship with the risen Christ. We should love, know and experience Jesus. As we have this experience the Holy Spirit bears witness within us. Jesus said, 'If any man will do his will, he shall know of the doctrine, whether it be of God.' If we earnestly want to know the truth, we will earnestly pray that God will reveal it to us, and He will not disappoint us.

Deliver us from evil. For those seeking release from bondage to the occult:

1. Apart from Christ you are without hope. ' "Salvation is found in no one else, for there is no other name under heaven given to men by which we must be saved." ' Acts 4:12, NIV. The positive truth, in the words of Jesus, is this, ' "I tell you the truth, whoever hears my word and believes him who sent me has eternal life and will not be condemned; he has crossed over from death to life." ' John 5:24, NIV.

Unless you are prepared to surrender your whole life,

body, mind and spirit to Jesus Christ you will never find the peace and the release you seek. Satan will seek to attract you as an angel of light, and ultimately blow your mind with terror and destruction.

The awesome witness of the Bible is this: 'For this purpose the Son of God was manifested, that he might destroy the works of the devil.' 1 John 3:8. Jesus died that 'he might destroy him who holds the power of death — that is, the devil'. Hebrews 2:14, NIV.

Satan is subtle. He seeks to misrepresent, caricature Christians. He wants to produce hybrid Christians with warped personalities. He wants to render Christians sterile. By thus 'infiltrating' phoneys into the Christian camp he can provide stumbling blocks to those who are perishing. He aims to rob Christians of the peace, joy and assurance that is their birthright. He wants to take away their freedom and destroy their relationship with the risen Christ. That is why Christians are constantly warned to walk according to the light (1 John 1:6, 7); to be on the alert (1 Peter 5:8); to 'put on the full armour of God so that you can take your stand against the devil's schemes' (Ephesians 6:11, NIV).

2. You must acknowledge that every involvement with the occult is, in fact, a pact with the devil. It gives him a legal right to bind and oppress you (Exodus 20:3-5). Playing around with a ouija board can be opening the door to the devil. The fact that you view it as a joke makes no difference to Satan. There is only one way to shut the door on the devil: Come to Jesus Christ in confession and renunciation.

The occultists in Ephesus who turned to Jesus 'came, confessing and divulging their practices' (Acts 19:18, RSV), renouncing the hidden things (2 Corinthians 4:2). Destroy occult objects (Acts 19:19). Before you pray spend time considering exactly what you want to confess.

Deliverance from demonic bondage is like our salvation. It is 'not of ourselves; it is the gift of God; not of works . . . ' (Ephesians 2:8, 9). It is not based on our merit. Not dependent on our feelings. Regardless of your emotional state at this point you have come before God with an open heart in confession. Hence you have the assurance of 1 John 1:9 that he is 'faithful and just to forgive us our sins, and to cleanse us from all unrighteousness.' The door has now been shut on Satan. Don't let him take away your faith in this fact.

3. End-time has arrived. The false christs and false prophets and false miracles prophesied are here.

The devil knows he has little time left. Nevertheless, however furious, however subtle the warfare, the believer who clings in obedience and faith to Jesus need *never* retreat in the face of the onslaught of demons. The one who, in obedience to God's command, puts the spirits to the test, cannot long be deceived.

Now, you must become an active warrior in these final days. Demons are in terror before the one who understands the victory and power of the blood of Christ. It is that blood which has shattered Satan's grasp upon us. To surrender in confession make sure at all times that you are 'washed in the blood of the Lamb'.

'Then I heard a loud voice in heaven say: "Now have come the salvation and the power and the kingdom of our God, and the authority of his Christ. For the accuser of our brothers, who accuses them before our God day and night, has been hurled down. They overcame him by the blood of the Lamb and by the word of their testimony.' Revelation 12:10, 11, NIV.

This is the greatest weapon God has given to us, the protection of the blood of the Lamb that cleanses us from all sin.

4. God has armour and requires us to wear it. No warrior goes into battle with only parts of his equipment. 'Put on the full armour of God so that you can take your stand against the devil's schemes. . . .' Ephesians 6:11, NIV.

Because 'our struggle is not against flesh and blood' but against 'the spiritual forces of evil' (Ephesians 6:12), the full armour of God is essential: Unless we wear the belt of truth our armour will not hold together; unless we have put on the breastplate of the righteousness of Christ, our heart can be pierced through with pride and self-righteousness; unless our feet are shod with the sturdy shoes of the Gospel of peace we can be thrown off balance by every stormy wind of doctrine that hits us; unless we take up the shield of faith, Satan's flaming missiles of doubt and temptation will lodge deep in our flesh and burn us. We need the helmet of salvation to guard our minds and the sword of the Spirit which is the living Word of God. This we alternately use to defend ourselves and to thrust forward.

Never underestimate the power of prayer and worship in the battle against Satan. Never underestimate God's power to defend those who have asked for His protection.

The devil is a beaten foe. He received a mortal wound in the battle fought on Calvary. The terror of the occult was robbed of its power by Calvary. In the words of Michael Green; 'Christ is the conqueror over all the power of the enemy, and on the cross He inflicted such a crushing defeat on the devil that whenever His name is named in faith, Satan is bound to flee.' Green then adds this testimony: 'I have seen this time and time again in lives afflicted by demonic possession. The demons have to leave when commanded to do so in the name of the Victor. That theme of Christ the Conqueror is one of the major ways in which the cross is seen in the New Testament.' *I Believe in Satan's Downfall* (Hodder and Stoughton).

But Satan is like the Axis forces in Europe in the second World War. The Normandy landings proved decisive for the outcome of the war. The final defeat for the Axis powers was inevitable. But the war went on. They refused to accept defeat. Sometimes a degree of success attended their struggles. Occasionally things looked favourable for them. But nothing could alter the fact that they were doomed. The ultimate Victory Day dawned in 1945.

That is how it is with Satan.

Revelation 12 and 13 present, at first glance, a chilling scenario. Before Christ returns in glory the devil will make one last stand. A final confrontation — a battle of Armageddon — will take place. There God will be victorious.

The end for the devil and his followers is certain. It will be in a lake of fire (Revelation 19:20; 20:10). The picture in Revelation, says Michael Green, 'denotes final and irreversible ruin and annihilation rather than endless torment'.

Nevertheless, the lake of fire will be the end of all devils and demons and those who have followed them.

A final word . . .

To the sad and the sorrowing I point to Jesus Christ, 'the Resurrection and the Life', through whose own resurrection the power of death has been broken and the choice made available to man — between eternal life and eternal oblivion. Though worms may destroy our earthly bodies, in our recreated flesh we shall meet the Lord when He returns in glory if, with the empty hand of faith, we have accepted His salvation.

To the fearful and the afraid I bid you place your trust in an all-sufficient God and I remind you of the words of a king and a prophet: 'Though I walk through the valley of the shadow of death, I will fear no evil: for thou art with me.' Psalm 23:4.

To those who feel the spine-chilling call to the world of the occult I would remind you of the all-destructive power of the alien force behind it all. I would remind you too of how it all started. And I would remind you of how it will end.

CHAPTER SEVENTEEN

NEW AGE: THE LAST DECEPTION?

Spirit guides. Channelling. Reincarnation. The glamour of superstars like Shirley Maclaine. The respectability of great performers like Sir Yehudi Menuhin.

The New Age deception has taken in hard-headed tycoons, ageing hippies, scientists and psychiatrists. It has adopted Christian terms — but made them mean something different. It has infiltrated thousands of Christian congregations and, in doing so, brought with it its own beliefs and supernatural, occult phenomena.

For reasons of its own it has pushed up front the belief that Jesus Christ will soon appear, in person, with His angels, for the benefit of 'the faithful'. . . .

The Findhorn connection. If the 'back of beyond' is a real place, it is near Findhorn.

Here, where ferocious seas lash themselves into a frenzy against the north coast of Scotland, is a community of upwards of 200. Dawns are pale and mist-wrapped at Findhorn. And the mist seems to shroud and permeate what was once the Cluny Hill Resort Hotel where the 200 plus live. Permeates even their thinking and their speaking. Making sense of the answers exchanged for my simple question, 'What is the New Age movement?' was rather like knitting fog. . . .

But with their vagueness came a courtesy which was positively disarming.

My impulse was to drive away, right foot on the floor, withdraw from this corner of the world where eyes looked past me, conversation seemed a thing impossible, and ultimate evil lowered over the place like an imminent storm.

But I squared my jaw. I was not about to be fazed by a shamble of pie-eyed professors and middle-aged hippies. I had information that this was where the New Age movement was nurtured, where everyone who was anyone in that movement came to spend time in indoctrination. If anyone could answer my question, it was somebody here.

A figure had detached itself from the group on the coast path.

I summoned up my courage. His waxy pallor was touched with acne, and his eyes, from their deep, bony sockets, stared beyond me.

I asked my question.

'The New Age', he purred in Californian tone. 'There is much you need to learn. . . .'

Then, as if with superhuman effort, he brought his brain into focus; 'You Christians belong to the past. Your age is fading. . . .'

Had I said I was a Christian? I mused. Crisping up he said, 'The Christian age has been the Age of Pisces. The age about to dawn is the Age of Aquarius. . . .'

A tune from the early seventies began to play in the back of my memory; '*It is the dawning of the Age of Aquarius. . . .*' It belonged to that psychedelic age of *Jesus Christ Superstar*, Richard Bach's *Jonathan Livingstone Seagull* and the spiced scents of Eastern religion brought West.

'Robert Runcie and John Stott have connected your "voices" and "channelling" with Satanism. . . ,' I blustered.

There was a preoccupied smile on his face. If he replied at all his words were lost on the sonorous boom of North Sea breakers. Gulls wheeled and screeched overhead. The lowering sky's dark shipping was coming together over Findhorn.

Despite the Findhorn connection, Englishman Will Baron — whose book *Deceived by the New Age* (Pacific Press) has done much to expose the movement glamorized by Shirley Maclaine — had to cross the Atlantic to encounter it.

Nevertheless, Djwhal Khul, channelling through Baron's

60-year-old mentor Muriel in a 'Lighted Way' meeting, had given direct instruction that he must return to Britain and spend time at Findhorn.

At this stage a channeller of Djwhal Khul himself, Baron had gone so far as to sell up all his possessions to return to Britain. That is where the 'Hierarchy of the Masters' wanted him to be.

He found a hotel in London. Weeks went by and the familiar depression settled upon him. Until, that is, the voice of 'God' blitzed him three times with the words 'Go forth in strength!' Each time the words were accompanied by a blast of energy. 'If I had not been sitting in a chair', writes Baron, 'the force of the energy might well have knocked me to the floor!'

Before driving north to Findhorn he visited Canterbury Cathedral. 'I recited occult prayers and invocations.' He visualized the great cathedral and its daughter churches being filled with the 'christ light' channelled by 'the Hierarchy of the Masters'. Visits to other great cathedrals followed. Occult prayers were said and, where opportunity permitted, pagan rites performed.

Then came the drive to Findhorn, what Baron described as 'the Vatican city of the New Age movement'. Four hundred people were to be present during his six-month stay. Findhorn was, he said, the 'prime New Age educational institution'.

As an 'insider' Baron's reception at and perception of Findhorn were very different from mine. 'This community is not a bunch of hippies,' he writes. 'Most of the people I met were university educated professionals.' He made many friends, among them a former Jesuit priest, a seminary professor and a number of men who at one time had been Bible teachers.

The central building contained eighty-seven rooms, looked like a castle and was equipped with every possible piece of state-of-the-art audio-visual equipment and the facilities of an efficient printing and publishing house.

It was in the publications department that Baron found

employment. For much of his stay he helped to publish a variety of New Age books, magazines and brochures. Baron participated in a number of supernatural happenings and became 'a full member' of the 'divine order'. This made him part of 'the world's foremost New Age organization'.

Alice Bailey and Ruth Montgomery. The New Agers' surrogate 'bible' are books written by Alice Bailey and Ruth Montgomery.

Like Will Baron in his early phase, Alice Bailey was a 'channel' for Djwhal Khul. After her death in 1949 Benjamin Creme assumed her function as the primary 'channel' of Djwhal Khul.

The mass following now enjoyed by the New Age movement developed in the late 60s and early 70s when Western values were abandoned and the Eastern religions came into vogue. It takes bits and pieces from Buddhism *and* Hinduism. Reincarnation and 'channelling' spirits from 'a higher evolutionary realm' are key concepts. The Findhorn community got under way in 1957 but was founded in its present form in 1970. Those resident there have always received regular spirit messages.

Whole bookshops in the USA, Germany and other countries in Central Europe are given over to New Age publications. Ruth Montgomery's books are unusual in that she claimed that they were actually written by 'the spirits'. One month after the death of American medium Arthur Ford, Ms. Montgomery describes how her hand was grasped by 'a force of herculean strength'. Ford's ashes had been scattered over the Atlantic but, claims Ms. Montgomery, he was now writing a book through her fingers. Its intent: to describe the after-life. Her function was to place a yellow sheet in her typewriter and sit for fifteen minutes a day while the dead psychic manipulated her fingers. It would appear that he typed his messages single-spaced, without punctuation or capitalization — and that his spelling was a great deal better than hers was!

In the after-life he had, he told Ruth Montgomery, rubbed shoulders with J. F. Kennedy, Winston Churchill and Marilyn

Monroe. He had not, however, run across either God or Jesus.

Soon the book, at just under six dollars, was a best-seller. It drove a coach and horses through previously-held beliefs about life after life. 'The man or woman who wishes to be assured that there is no death, no hell, no judgement, and no devil to worry about', writes George Vandeman in *Psychic Roulette* (Thomas Nelson), 'would find the book comforting. The man who doesn't want God looking over his shoulder, either now or later, the man who would prefer a future life in which both God and Jesus keep themselves out of sight, and so remote as to scarcely intrude even upon his thoughts — that man would be reassured.'

But this was only one book that emerged through Ruth Montgomery's fingers. Others written by 'spirit guides' describe how the New Age will begin. The 'enlightened ones' (New Age believers) will be evacuated from the earth by rescue ships in space. . . .

Helen Schucman also claims to have a spirit-driven type-writer. In a 1,100-page book she claims to be a 'channel' for the 'spirit' of 'Jesus'. The central claim of the book is that He is not the Son of God.

Nevertheless, the books of Shirley Maclaine have done most for her publishers: Bantam Books. They include *Out on a Limb*, *Dancing in the Light*, *You Can Get There From Here*, and *Going Within*.

While being the best-known channeller of all, Ms. Maclaine does not claim that her books were written by any-one other than herself. The theme that runs through them all is that 'everyone is God — everyone'. In *Dancing in the Light* she says, 'I know that I exist, therefore I am. I know that the godsource exists, therefore it is. Since I am a part of that force, I am that I AM.' (In making this claim Ms. Maclaine is assuming the most sacred name of God.) The basic human predicament, she claims, is not moral (sin and guilt), but ignorance of our true identity. We are not alienated from God, but from our true selves. What we need, she argues, is not forgiveness but enlightenment.

CHAPTER EIGHTEEN

THE SEDUCTION OF CHRISTIANITY

The most outspoken opponents of the New Age have been two British churchmen, Robert Runcie and John Stott.

Both men have contributed lengthy, well-researched articles to a long series published by *Christian Week* and the *Church of England Newspaper*.

'The New Age movement is difficult to pin down, hard to identify, . . .' writes Runcie. 'It is an all-embracing term for no single phenomenon. . . . Saying anything too precise about the New Age movement is liable to give it a coherence which it does not possess.'

'Infatuation with self'. 'From beginning to end the New Age movement expresses a preoccupation and even infatuation with self, . . .' writes Dr. Stott. 'It puts the self in the place of God and even declares that we *are* God. New Agers have surrendered to the primeval temptation to be like God, as in the Garden of Eden. God is effectively dethroned.'

'The so-called "New Age" movement', asserts Stott, 'is both a counterfeit and a fraud. . . . '

Introducing 'the dangers of the New Age' in *Christian Weekly* John Martin and Andrew Carey write, 'Vast numbers of Christians are blissfully unaware of the existence of the so-called "New Age" movement. That in itself is very dangerous.'

They argue that New Agers reject entirely the Judaeo-Christian tradition and any conception of 'a personal, loving God, a fallen humanity, or a crucified and risen Christ'. They warn, 'The religious sections of high street bookshops are crammed with books on I Ching Buddhism, crystals and New Age paraphernalia. Even some reputable bookshops have theology sections dominated by the occult. . . . Soap operas on prime time television popularize seance sessions and fortune telling.'

Rowena White calls New Age 'designer religion'. 'You take the more enticing bits of Eastern religions like reincarnation, pantheism, meditation, mix in a few crystals, alternative medicine, health food, and read Shirley Maclaine, and it's all perfectly respectable and credible.' This is why, she argues, New Age has appealed to yuppies rather than cranky fringe elements. New Age magazines are easily mistaken for environmental magazines, and to be environment-friendly is to be a 'happening person'. But from ecology, alternative medicine, homeopathy, New Agers find it a short hop to direct occult involvement.

Ms. White continues: 'We need to test the spirits (1 John 4:1-3), and be alert for false prophets (2 Peter 2:1), because error is often very close to the truth, but it is still error. Most of all, we need to be firmly rooted in the Gospel, to know what we believe and what is the foundation of our faith, so we are able to give a reason for the hope we have (1 Peter 3:15) and so that we know the answers when the old enemy in a new guise asks, "Did God *really* say . . . ?" '

Robert Runcie was often accused of 'fudging issues'. Not so with the New Age. He listed fertility cults, primal religions, Satanism and witchcraft among the sources of New Age beliefs and practices.

The New Age and the Bible. The New Age 'channels' contradict the Bible on many important points. The following list — by no means exhaustive — is drawn from the series in *Christian Week* to which Robert Runcie and John Stott were the main contributors, and from an authoritative analysis of New Age representing a decade's full-time study; Kenneth Wade's, *Secrets of the New Age* (Review and Herald).

1. The channels teach that there are many 'christs'. The Bible teaches that Jesus is the unique Son of God who came to earth to live and die once for all humanity.

2. Some of the channels teach that there is no such thing as the devil; others that he is a good angel who has had

a bad press from the Bible. The Bible reveals Satan as the originator of sin and deception, and the enemy of all who want to live God's way.

3. The channels teach that there is no such thing as absolute truth. The Bible reveals Jesus as the Way, the Truth and the Life. It also recalls Jesus' promise that 'you will know the truth, and the truth will set you free' (John 8:32, NIV).

4. The channels teach that the 'inner self' of a human being is 'God'. The Bible makes a distinction between the creature and the Creator. It asserts that only those who receive Jesus Christ as Saviour and Lord will be saved in God's Kingdom.

5. The channels teach that man, unaided, has the power to be perfect and make a perfect world. The Bible reveals man as helpless, powerless to do good. The Bible's promise is that through God's grace and the power of His Spirit man can develop an unselfish character in an imperfect world.

6. The channels place their hope for a better future in the New Age and a spaceship evacuation from the planet. The Bible's hope for a better future is based on Christ's promise to return.

7. The channels teach cosmic evolution; the Bible teaches fiat creation.

8. The channels teach that, through evolution over billions of years, the spirits who channel messages to man are beings who have reached a higher evolved state. The Bible teaches that, because of sin and the Fall, man has deteriorated and is in need of 'salvation'.

9. Channels teach that a New Age is about to dawn, and will result in beings attaining to a higher level still. The Bible teaches that the world will come to an end and that at that time Jesus Christ will return in a visible manner that no one will be able to ignore, and that He will then establish His eternal kingdom of righteousness.

10. Channels all teach reincarnation, that there is no such thing as death. The Bible teaching on death is that it is a sleep from which men will be resurrected at the second

advent of Christ and that, at some time thereafter, they will face judgement.

Tony Higton, examining the evidence for New Age infiltration into the church in *Christian Week*, sees the second chapter of the second letter of Peter as being of great importance.

Peter provides a graphic description of the false teachers of his day. Higton points out some similarities between those false teachers and the New Age channellers:

1. Heresy can often be very subtle (verse 1). Pantheism is just one example of what can emerge from a 'creation-centred spirituality'.

2. False teaching can give the entire church a 'bad press' (verse 2). Consider the impact of the 'name it and claim it' prosperity gospel of some of the American TV evangelists and the dire consequences.

3. Greed can often be a motive (verse 3). New Age industry, including music, has mushroomed into multi-million-pound marketing concerns.

4. One mark of heresy is that it is often arrogant, blasphemous, and ignorant both of the holiness and providence of God (verse 10).

5. Another is that it is self-centred (verse 13). Much New Age thought is self-centred, making the 'self' the centre of the universe.

6. Most heresies promise freedom but in the end cause bondage (verse 19).

What about infiltration? Will Baron provides evidence of wholesale infiltration of Christian congregations in Califonia.

The excesses of the Episcopal cathedral of St. John the Divine in New York have been well documented as examples of how the Christian church is highly susceptible to New Age infiltration — even manipulation.

Concern has been expressed in Church of England publications with regard to the nature of Creation Festivals convened in a number of cathedrals, including Salisbury, Coventry and Bristol. Even greater concern has been expressed that St. James's, Piccadilly, is actually used as a place of New Age worship. Christian leaders in Germany have done their homework and provided themselves with concrete reasons for concern. They have found evidence of 70,000 New Age groups meeting on a weekly basis. . . . .

Tony Higton in the *Church of England Newspaper* expresses deep concern at New Age infiltration into Christian congregations. He emphasizes the New Age concern to camouflage its 'occult connections'. 'It is', he says, 'actually closely connected with Spiritualism and witchcraft, and only a short step from Satanism.'

Higton expresses the belief that the mainstream Anglican communion has been infiltrated by the New Age concept of *syncretism*,* a belief fundamental to Hinduism. Sentimental Anglicans are in a special danger from a syncretistic attitude; 'People of other religions are so nice, so devout. They put us Christians to shame. They can't be without God and without hope. Surely they're taking their different way to God . . . .'

Higton emphasizes the ambivalence of Dr. Runcie on syncretism. He points out that on occasion Runcie has warned against the syncretistic nature of the New Age movement. And yet that, on other occasions, he has spoken *very* positively of other religions as 'genuine mansions of the Spirit'. He quotes Runcie as having said, 'We will have to abandon any narrowly conceived Christian apologetic, based on a sense of superiority and an exclusive claim to truth.' With some concern he cites an example in which Dr. Runcie quoted, with approval, Arnold Toynbee, that the twentieth century would be remembered 'as the time when the first sign became visible of that great interpretation of Eastern religions and Christianity which gave rise to the great universal religion of the third millennium AD.'

Apparently the thought-forms of even some Christian opponents of the New Age are, to a degree, moulded by New Age concepts. . . .

---

* Attempted reconciliation of conflicting or opposite beliefs.

CHAPTER NINETEEN

THE COUNTERFEIT CHRIST

But there is more to the New Age infiltration of the Christian church than syncretism.

What about the claim that certain New Age influenced TV evangelists and 'Christian' preachers have been 'taken over'? And the confident assertion of such preachers that Jesus Christ and His angels will soon appear in physical form to selected convocations of the faithful?

For starters Christians should not be surprised at either the assertion or the phenomenon, if and when it appears. Jesus plainly warned that He would be impersonated in 'the last days'. He said, ' "At that time if anyone says to you, 'Look, here is the Christ!' or 'There he is!' do not believe it. For false Christs and false prophets will appear and perform great signs and miracles to deceive even the elect — if that were possible. See, I have told you ahead of time. So if anyone tells you, 'There he is, out in the desert,' do not go out; or, 'Here he is, in the inner rooms,' do not believe it. For as the lightning comes from the east and flashes to the west, so will be the coming of the Son of Man.'' ' Matthew 24:23-27, NIV.

It's now eight years since I was taken aback by a full-page ad in my sober-sides newspaper. The ad announced: 'The Christ is here.' The Christ had, apparently, already arrived and had met with a select few. Within the next eighteen days, we were warned, he would appear physically on the streets of our cities, visible for all to see. The same ad was carried by every other major newspaper on the same day. Upon enquiry it was found to have been placed — at fantastic cost — by Benjamin Creme who, it will be recalled, had succeeded Alice Bailey as the primary 'channel' of Djwhal Khul. The eighteen days passed, and there were no reports of 'sightings'.

But what if 'Christ' *had* appeared, say, in some great convocation of the cults, or in a charismatic convention — or in the middle of Oxford Street or Times Square?

Even the hard-boiled classes would have to sit up and take notice. And let's be quite clear, such a counterfeit would be child's play for the archdemon who has already most impressively impersonated Christ repeatedly to, among thousands of others, Johanna Michaelsen, Will Baron and Will Baron's mentor Muriel.

'He stood there right in the middle of my locked bedroom,' Muriel had said. 'And he told me to get down on my knees. If people think that Jesus is a weedy weakling, they are in for a big surprise. He is over six feet tall and looks very dignified and handsome. He is a power-r-r-ful being. . . . I got out of bed and knelt in front of Jesus. He laid his hands upon my head and gave me a blessing. Then he turned around and walked straight through the solid, locked door of my hotel room. . . . '

The large-scale infiltration of Christian congregations in which Will Baron was one of thousands of carefully prepared, indoctrinated participants — what would be the point of it?

Could it be that the evil forces in the dark world of the occult are planning one final hoax to confuse, divide and 'if it were possible' (Matthew 24:24) destroy the Christian church? Or, at the very least, draw away thousands, perhaps millions — before the second coming of the *real* Jesus Christ occurs?

'After becoming Christians, many who have been involved in the New Age movement and know it from the inside, enquire why they find much of the same occultism in the church and on Christian TV and why very few pastors seem willing to be able to confront this issue. There is a growing grass roots concern that most Christian television in North America is controlled by a handful of people who have the final say on all programming. They wield great power and influence, yet are insulated from any correction from the . . . body of Christ and are accountable to no one but themselves. The same thing applies to the spreading Christian satellite network. . . .' Dave Hunt and T. A. McMahon, *The Seduction of Christianity* (Harvest House).

Can you see how it could happen?

The present occult upsurge can be traced to the rappings on the wall of that wooden shack in Hydesville. If rappings in an isolated shack have led to the psychic thunder of today, what would be the result of a phenomenon far grander — and witnessed by multitudes?

Is the ultimate hoax round the corner? Is this what the New Age upsurge in the Western world is all about?

It would appear that we have arrived at a time when we can no longer trust our own senses. No longer believe what our eyes and our ears tell us. A time when miracles can lie. A time when we need some more reliable yardstick than our own judgement. A time when the counterfeit will so closely resemble the real that it will be impossible to distinguish just where error diverges from truth except by divine revelation. A time when the archdemon is working with 'all kinds of counterfeit miracles, signs and wonders' (2 Thessalonians 2:9, NIV).

The world has been made ready for a monstrous deception. The subtle but powerful softening of the minds of men and the infiltration of Christianity is not without purpose.

One leading New Ager has actually recorded a voice purporting to be from a spaceship hovering above the earth. It is a voice that makes your spine tingle — the sweetest voice you ever heard. And it says, 'My little children, I am about to return according to my promise.' George Vandeman, *Psychic Roulette*, pages 162, 163.

What is planned is no crude or clumsy delusion. It is something big. Big enough, in fact, to deceive almost everybody. Everybody, that is, who is not fortified with knowledge obtained from Scripture of the *manner* in which the real Christ will come. For when the real Christ descends from skies full-brilliant with angels the spectacle will be visible from east to west, as visible as the lightning. Every eye in the world will be watching as He comes close to the earth, calls the dead to life, and catches His people up to meet Him — without His feet ever touching the earth. God will permit Satan to go a long way with his tricks and his games. But He will never permit him to duplicate the *way* in which the Son of God returns to the earth.

The New Age has created a climate in which thousands are ready to believe anything that smacks of the supernatural. And those who scoff at the ghoulies and ghosties and things that go bump in the night are just as easily snared. For their scoffing has left them unprepared. They will find out too late that devils can work miracles after all.

Who is safe? Not many. Only those who have read the Book, and believed it more than their eyes and their ears — even when the storm seemed to be sweeping everything away.

Meanwhile over Findhorn a black cloud-mountain threatens a nerve-shattering storm. And in the drawing rooms vacuous stares are replaced with the glint of excitement. They are preparing one final deception.

CHAPTER TWENTY

GOD'S EMPIRE STRIKES BACK

The Fox sisters were in at the birth of Spiritualism in 1844. The first demonic message was: 'Dear friends . . . . You must proclaim these truths to the world. This is the dawning of a new era, and you must not try to conceal it any longer. . . . ' Cited, Russ Parker, *The Occult: Deliverance From Evil* (IVP).

So, when it comes down to it, what's 'new' about New Age?

New Age so called was already thousands of years old when the Fox sisters worked out their Morse code with the devil. It began close to the dawn of time and is built on lies Lucifer let loose in Eden.

The story is told in Genesis chapter 3.

Back then the fallen Lucifer chose to channel through a serpent. The first words channelled — ' "*Did God really say . . . ?*" ' (verse 1, NIV) — were the beginning of all evil, all tragedy, all death on the planet. Their objective: to instil doubt about what God said. Their inference: 'God doesn't *really* love you. He's holding something back.'

Believe that God loves you personally and you are invincible to the assaults of Satan. Evil begins when the love of God is questioned.

The voice of the archdemon droned on through his chosen channel: ' "*You will not surely die. . . .* " ' (Verse 4, NIV.) This is the central heresy of the New Age movement. Elizabeth Kubler-Ross believes everyone will be in heaven; including Adolf Hitler and Joseph Stalin. New Age says, 'Because we're God, we cannot die. We live on in a new form.' Some in the spooky world of the spirits. Others being 'recycled' — reincarnated — again and again until, having paid for all their failures and mistakes, having worked off all their *karma*, they drop into the ocean of the infinite (*Nirvana*), final extinction, part of universal god.

The channeller's voice went on: ' *"You will be like God, knowing good and evil."* ' (Verse 4, NIV.) The New Age promises 'to open your eyes' to esoterica, elevate you to new planes of awareness. 'Through trance-meditation,' say the channellers, 'through yoga, through drugs — your eyes will be opened.'

That's what Esoteric Mike told Greta (see Chapter 1) and, instead of opening her eyes, increasing her awareness, a combination of occult-induced depression and drugs killed her. Over six years she had been taught to turn her back on the Judaeo-Christian system of ethics, and told 'You are a god. You decree what is good and evil for yourself. Whatever feels good: do it.'

But everything we do meets us again. Every choice is important. Greta acknowledged this to Kevin Logan during rare moments of consciousness in her last seven days of life. But for her it was too late.

The heart of the New Age heresy is: 1. That man is God; 2. That man has the resources within himself to achieve perfection and ultimate fulfilment.

1. **Is man God?** At the beginning of all things man was made in the 'image' of God (Genesis 1:26, 27.) But any character resemblance between Creator and creature was largely destroyed at the Fall. The Fall broke us into a thousand pieces spiritually. Our thoughts are full of garbage: fears, doubts, criticisms, lusts. And the New Age movement wants us to believe that *we* are gods . . . ?

Because of sin we are marred, spoiled, lost. We need redemption, re-creation, new birth. We are creatures dependent upon our Creator for our every breath, and on our Redeemer for rescue from the pit of sin.

'At just the right time, when we were still powerless, Christ died for the ungodly. . . . For just as through the disobedience of the one man the many were made sinners, so also through the obedience of the one man the many will be made righteous.' Romans 5:6, 19, NIV.

2. **What is man?** The New Age teaches that man can achieve ultimate perfection. What is the Bible view of the nature of man? His heart is calloused and most of the time he goes through life neither hearing nor seeing (Acts 28:27). Separated from God, man's heart is hardened by ignorance (Ephesians 4:18). Separated from God, men are like sheep, astray in the wilderness with no homing instinct (Isaiah 53:6). Left to himself, man is naturally hostile to both good and God (Romans 8:7). To understand spiritual reality man is 100 per cent dependent on God (1 Corinthians 2:9-14). Men's ' "throats are open graves; their tongues practise deceit. The poison of vipers is on their lips" ' (Romans 3:13). Man's natural tendency is to sluggishness, inactivity and total lack of imagination (Proverbs 21:25). Sin sucks man down like a whirlpool; only God can rescue him (Ephesians 2:1, 2). 'The heart is deceitful above all things and beyond cure. Who can understand it?' Jeremiah 17:9, NIV.

Without God man is mired in sin. Sin renders man helpless. Sin is madness in the brain, poison in the heart, a tornado on the loose, a gangster on the prowl, lightning streaking towards earth, a terminal cancer eating its way into the souls of men, a raging torrent that sweeps everything before it.

Because of sin every stream is stained with human crime, every breeze is morally corrupted, every day's light is blackened, every life's cup is tainted, every life's roadway is made hazardous with pitfalls. Sin destroys happiness, darkens the understanding, seers the conscience, withers everything, causes all tears of sorrow, pangs of agony. It promises velvet but gives a shroud; promises liberty but delivers bondage; promises nectar but serves up gall. Sin breaks hearts, blights homes and robs heaven. It is the most devastating fact about the universe. *But the New Age does not mention sin.*

There is only one way to be delivered from sin, the occult and the New Age: to acknowledge our need and to fall at the feet of Jesus Christ.

Jesus. New Age guru and Findhorn chief-of-operations David Spangler has written: 'Jesus merely built upon the pattern that Buddha had established. . . . As a child He differed but little from other children only that in past lives He had overcome carnal propensities.'

Founder of Scientology — an aspect of the New Age against which both the British and Australian governments have legislated — L. Ron Hubbard has written: 'Christ is just above clear.' In the jargon of Scientology, L. Ron Hubbard is saying that Jesus was free of 'engrams' (problems) but, by implication, significantly spiritually inferior to L. Ron Hubbard!

What *is* the *real* nature of the Man who claimed to be God?

Jesus was the *only* Man who claimed to be God and was thought sane by the best and the wisest of his contemporaries. Buddha, Mohammed, Zoroaster and the rest never claimed to be God.

Today no accepted historian doubts the historicity of Christ. Outside the New Testament it is ironic that the evidence for His existence comes from the records and histories of those who sought to destroy Christianity in the early centuries: the Jews and the Romans. No accredited scholar questions the authenticity of the writings of Josephus, the *Talmud*, Suetonius, Tacitus and Pliny the Younger — all provide evidence of Christ and the early growth of Christianity.

It would, in any event, have taken a Christ to have invented the Christ. His words in the gospels provide their own authentication. The unadorned gospel records of Matthew, Mark, Luke and John also are self-authenticating. The record of the crucifixion is the most unadorned record of tragedy that exists in all literature. The record was written in such a way that we know it could not have been contrived. The New Testament writers are unashamedly frank whatever the cost to the reputations of those who, after the resurrection, led the Christian cause.

He lived. The manuscripts are reliable. But what sort of claims did Christ make?

'All power is given unto me in heaven and in earth.' Matthew 28:18. Notice, this Galilean carpenter is not saying, 'I am the King of the Jews.' He is saying, 'I am Almighty God.'

Confronted at His trial with the question, 'Are you the Son of God?' Jesus answered, 'I am: and ye shall see the Son of man sitting on the right hand of power, and coming in the clouds of heaven.' Mark 14:62.

In Matthew 9:2 He claimed to have the power to forgive sin. In Mark 4:39 He claimed the power to control the elements. In Matthew 25:31, 32 He claimed to be the judge of all the earth; 'When the Son of man shall come in his glory, and all the holy angels with him, then shall he sit upon the throne of his glory: and before him shall be gathered all nations. . . . '

C. S. Lewis was correct with regard to the claims of Jesus. He said that, given such claims, Jesus had to be mad or bad — or God. No one, apparently, is suggesting that He was mad or bad. True enough, some have made the claim that He was 'simply a great teacher'. But how *could* He have been — making such claims? He did not leave us that option. He was mad, or bad, or . . . .

His life so matched His words that His words carry a self-authenticating power. When we hear Him say, 'Come unto me all who are weary and heavy burdened,' no irony strikes us. A penniless artisan — inviting all the world to bring their burdens and place them on His shoulders. It doesn't strike us as strange because His life was such that His deeds matched His words. The most natural explanation of Christ's life is the supernatural: if He was good, He was God.

Jesus and the good news. Jesus summarized His message and mission in these words: '*God so loved the world that he gave his one and only Son, that whoever believes in him shall not perish but have eternal life.*' John 3:16, NIV.

Christians believe that that text is chock-full of significant truth. That to understand it and believe it brings transformation, joy and heaven.

It affirms that we are not clinging to a runaway planet; God is in control. It affirms that man has become bad and needs changing. It warns that a judgement day is coming, and only those found in Christ will survive that day. It promises that this world will not always be the lazar-house of suffering it now is, nor the rubbish dump sin has made it, for everlasting life is to displace the reign of sorrow and death. And more yet — it sets out in simple terms the 'how' of salvation; *that whoever believes in him . . . '*.

The greatest of the apostles, Paul, set out in comprehensive detail what 'believing' entails.

If you believe you will come to Christ as you are, with all your guilt and sin — and pray for His forgiveness. And the good news is that at the very moment anyone puts his trust in Christ, he is freed from all condemnation — past, present and to come (for as long as he believes, despite a thousand falls and failures). His sins are not laid to his charge.

In Paul's letters the meaning of the death and resurrection of Jesus becomes clear. God 'made him to be sin for us, who knew no sin; that we might be made the righteousness of God in him' (2 Corinthians 5:21). His hands were pierced because of the wrong things our hands have done. . . . Isaiah says, 'He was pierced for our transgressions, he was crushed for our iniquities; the punishment that brought us peace was upon him, and by his wounds we are healed.' (53:5, NIV.)

The sin question — what New Agers call *karma* — is not solved by successive lifetimes in which it is 'worked out'. There is one lifetime. One period of probation in which all decisions have to be taken.

Man is sinful. The penalty of the broken law which is as sacred as God Himself has to be paid. *And it has been paid*. It was paid at 3pm Black Friday AD 31 by our Representative. 'We are convinced that one has died for all; therefore all have died.' 2 Corinthians 5:14, RSV.

When we 'believe in Him' we accept His sacrifice on Calvary as having been for us. We accept Him as our personal Saviour, our Representative. *He* paid *our* penalty.

Because of the life and death of Jesus, the sin question has become the Son question. 'Whoever believes in him is not condemned, but whoever does not believe stands condemned already. . . . ' John 3:18, NIV. Through the message of Jesus we hear the peal of gospel bells — and the roll of a fearful thunder. ' "I tell you the truth, unless a man is born again, he cannot see the kingdom of God." ' John 3:3, NIV. The great imperative: *'You must be born again.'*

Here Jesus asserts that without transformation of heart no man will live for ever. And that transformation, that rebirth, was not a one-off experience. It depended on maintaining a day-by-day, ongoing relationship with the risen Jesus.

It involved, day by day, making a total surrender to Him; day by day, surrendering sin and guilt and accepting pardon and righteousness; day by day, renouncing the past and embracing the future; day by day denying self and reaching out to Him, His infinite power.

'Whoever believes on him.' If you accept Him, yours are the doing and dying of Jesus — as though you had lived His life and died His death. Your sins are credited to Him when you confess them; the account was settled before you were born. Because of Calvary His righteousness can be credited to you.

' "Salvation is found in no one else, for there is no other name under heaven given to men by which we must be saved." ' Acts 4:12, NIV.

All the rest is deception; the deceptions in infinite variety contrived and executed by a subtle and malignant enemy, and updated with each new generation. However, though the terminology changes, though the 'crafts' change, and the emphases shift, it is all based on the lies that fallen Lucifer channelled through the serpent at time's dawn.

The deception was foretold that we might be forewarned. Foretold by Jesus Himself in the Olivet sermon (Matthew 24;

Mark 13; Luke 21). Foreshadowed by John in his first letter and by Paul in his two letters to the Thessalonians. Then set out in vivid technicolour in John's Revelation, the last book in Scripture.

The scenario again.

An end-time crisis in which 'false Christs and false prophets' will appear, all manner of miracles be worked by angels-turned-demons, and an attempt be made by the archdemon to fake the return of Jesus.

Then, the main event: *the day He comes.*

Jesus returning through full-brilliant skies so that 'every eye shall see him'. Returning to reward the second born, those who have 'believed' in His sacrifice for sin and been covered with His righteousness.

Finally, the judgement. Outside God's great city, the devil and every demon, together with the deceivers and deceived of every age — including 'those who practise magic arts' — 'devoured' by 'fire — from heaven' (Revelation 20:9; 21:8; 22:15, NIV).

New Ager Aldous Huxley in *Brave New World* described a world-in-the-future in which everyone would be on drugs, 'soma'. Aldous was the atheist grandson of Thomas Huxley, the nineteenth-century champion of Charles Darwin.

Aldous Huxley had been heavily into drugs, the New Age, and various forms of the occult.

In the final hours of his life his wife tape-recorded his last words: 'The whole thing has been very strange. In a way it was good; but in a way it was absolutely terrifying — showing that when one thinks one's got beyond oneself, one hasn't. I began with this marvellous sense of this cosmic gift; and then ended up with the rueful sense that one can be deceived. It was the most dangerous of errors inasmuch as one was worshipping oneself.' Huxley was a broken, bitter, disappointed man, typical of many who leave it too late to discover the truth behind the occult.

No one has ever been disappointed with Jesus.